# The Art of BONSAI

## Peter D. Adams

WARD LOCK

Text © Peter D. Adams 1981
Illustrations © Ward Lock Limited 1981

First published in Great Britain in 1981
by Ward Lock Limited, 41-47 Strand,
London WC2N 5JE, England
A Cassell Imprint

Reprinted 1982, 1984, 1986, 1988, 1989

2nd edition 1990

First paperback of 2nd edition 1992

Reprinted 1993

House editors Denis Ingram and Deborah Maby
Layout by Sheila Sherwen

Text filmset in Plantin Light
by MS Filmsetting Limited, Frome, Somerset

Printed and bound in Hong Kong by
Wing King Tong Co. Ltd.

CIP data for this book is available upon application
from The British Library.

ISBN 0-7063-7116-X

# Contents

**Dedication**

This book is dedicated to my wife, Sheila.

# Preface

Bonsai may be expressed as the controlled unfolding of the form of a tree in an idealized state. Working within limits of container and height, imposed by plant health on the one hand and accepted standards on the other, the grower seeks to reproduce the impression of a giant tree.

A good Bonsai is one that successfully conveys the image of a mature tree, but which on inspection, proves to be a physical abbreviation and an artistic expression of the species in nature. The magnetic charm of the classical Bonsai is achieved through the use of techniques that are effected for both horticultural and aesthetic reasons. The trained or experienced Bonsai designer will, when seeing a Bonsai, immediately recognize the various steps involved in its creation and, equally, when envisaging a new design, will quite unconsciously select the relevant techniques. The aim of the book is to make the process used by the designer quickly available, or at least to initiate that process.

The opening chapter entitled Preparation Techniques outlines the basic elements of the best contemporary design and describes the technical methods used, while Chapter 3 amplifies the specific techniques. Combining the two provides one with a framework within which to experiment. The styles are in no sense rigid: they are beautiful structures that complement to the fullest extent the qualities of various species. The descriptions in Chapter 1 deal in principles, and as far as space permits, the nuances of each style, but one must not neglect to study the Japanese classics which illustrate every sort of interpretation, variation and original concept suggested by the particular tree and will quickly generate all sorts of new possibilities and fresh ideas.

Similarly, the insistence on visual memory and the chapter on Aesthetics with its esoteric terms such as 'visual speed' are to help the student when confronted with the pure design aspects of Bonsai. Once these elusive properties can be identified and recognized, they may be utilized to give substance and satisfaction to the design. Only the broadest mention can be made of the artistic qualities of Bonsai, a host of other details appear with study, as does the mental picture gallery used by the experienced designer to dream up his new images.

The sections on Design Assessment and Evolution in Design illustrate through critique and actual example, the results, freedom and confidence in future planning, gained through the advocated systems.

The book is in seven parts for ease of reference and, although separately presented, the components are all of equal importance.

Finally I should like to thank Dan Barton, accomplished Bonsai grower and fellow enthusiast, for taking all the photographs used in this book.

P.D.A.

## Acknowledgements

All half-tone photographs and all colour photographs were taken by Dan Barton, A.I.I.P. of Bristol.

All line drawings are by the author.

The tree shown in Colour Plate 11 belongs to Dave Claridge. The trees shown in Colour Plates 16 and 42 belong to Dan Barton. The tree shown in colour plates 74–80 belongs to Bill Jordan and was styled by the author. All other trees are owned and styled by the author.

# Introduction

## BASIC DEFINITION OF BONSAI

The techniques of Bonsai as we know them today are logical extensions and adaptions of those mechanically applied by nature in the formation of natural Bonsai. The natural forces at work are those of climate, exposure and the element of inhospitable soil, all of which detract from the full performance of the tree.

CLIMATE Prevailing winds control the shapes of trees on exposed sites causing re-alignments and adaptions in an effort to streamline the shape, and conserve foliage moisture. Think of trees on the coast that grow away from onshore winds. Frost, snow and drought also cause shape adjustments through die-back, weight and the shedding of limbs in the effort to maintain moisture, and retard growth in the process.

EXPOSURE Trees are very affected by another factor, altitude. The higher the tree grows the dwarfer the habit through ultraviolet saturation.

SOIL Starved, either very porous, or very wet soil, all limit root growth and retard height.

The finest living example of trees on which all the techniques (except soggy soil) have been applied by nature must be the Bristle Cone Pines in the White Mountains on the California/Nevada border. Thousands of years old, the trees are only feet high. Rainfall is limited to approximately six weeks a year and therefore growth is very slow. Prevailing winds scour the trunks with sand, and every tree is a masterpiece of Sharimiki and Jin on the windward side, with all the foliage borne in the lee. At 12,000 feet the ultraviolet factor is immensely potent and every tree is compact with neat foliage. Soil is ultra-porous, being largely Dolomitic limestone shingle.

Smaller versions of the process are found and collected throughout the world and often need very little shaping, if any, to become truly impressive Bonsai with tapered, characterful trunks and branching. Most of the classics have been developed from natural Bonsai.

## The process

The rules of natural dwarfing are utilized by the grower in the development and maintenance of Bonsai.

ROOT PRUNING The plant is root pruned to remove the heavy portions of the system. This limits the tree because root and branch spread mirror each other. Root pruning also revitalizes the tree, creating a concentration of energy and this is reflected above and below in the dense growth of fine roots and branches.

SOIL The perfect Bonsai soil is one that is well drained and ventilated. Soils are sieved when dry to free them of fine particles. The ideal mixture is granular, light and nutritious and roots spread rapidly through such a molecular structure and cannot drown. Their activity is reflected overhead.

POT The tree is grown in a pot big enough to function adequately as a moisture reservoir but shallow enough to counterpoint the tree aesthetically. Drainage holes must operate perfectly.

PRUNING AND SHAPING The limbs are pruned to induce dwarfness, promote density, maintain the essential balance with the roots, and ventilate the interior tree, so air and light can keep all parts equally healthy. Trees are strongest at their apexes so pruning is adjusted accordingly, being deepest at the tip and lightest at the base. Pruning also achieves shaping which is further assisted through wire coiling, producing bends and curves to preconceived patterns.

EXPOSURE Bonsai are grown in pots on elevated shelves with full sun exposure. The ultraviolet action helps neaten foliage texture and the passage of drier air and light strengthens the tree.

WATERING Enough water is given to keep the plant constantly moist – not soggy. During windy or hot weather, soil watering is supplemented with foliar spray given after sundown.

FEEDING This varies according to the point of evolution: older trees are given enough to maintain their health but younger plants, like humans, need more. Feed is given on a regular basis from March to August.

PLACEMENT Bonsai are *outdoor* plants. Bonsai may be displayed indoors for short periods – one or two days at the most – but must have outdoor conditions for health: ventilation, seasonal change and good light. If trees *must* be brought indoors in leaf, limit the period to half a day for safety. In dormancy this factor is less critical – up to two days is permissible – but spray foliage, keep away from central heating and maintain light levels. When temperature differentials are marked cool the tree off in a frost-free acclimatization area before returning to its usual winter position.

# 1 Preparation techniques

The natural ability that the Japanese possess for presenting the essence of composition in delightfully proportioned ways is known throughout most of their art forms. This is never better expressed than in Bonsai. Their outlook has led, particularly over the last few decades, to certain styles or standard arrangements being recognized as the media in which given species are best expressed. It is the trees themselves that suggest the styles and the Japanese have found methods of accentuating these desirable effects.

Bonsai are strongly three-dimensional forms. Appreciation of the spatial aspects of Bonsai can add immeasurably to the immediate success of any contemplated design from Mame or miniature Bonsai to a three-foot giant. Bonsai arranged three dimensionally in styles suited to the species will in no time give the grower something of the satisfaction of the subject. Conversely, trees roughly planted together in an unsuitable pot can never really satisfy the grower or the observer. There are far too many such pseudo-Bonsai to be seen for it to be accidental. I do not just mean the inferior Japanese commercial Bonsai which, though mutilated by careless treatment, nonetheless often provide a good potential structure, or the genetic dwarf evergreens now claimed as Bonsai by some, but rather the dumb acceptance of that which at best can only argue sketchy appreciation of real Bonsai. There is no real excuse for these low standards when better things are so easily attainable. All one has to do is follow certain well-defined criteria, but more importantly, one has to develop a sense of visual memory which will also help in the analysis of design.

Visual memory is the key to understanding the Bonsai masterpiece and is a prerequisite for the Bonsai artist. This memory may be acquired and stimulated in a number of ways but by far the easiest method is by pictorial reference.

## Photographs
There are some excellent photo albums issued, such as the Nippon Bonsai Association album of the exhibit at Ueno Park which appears annually. These may be ordered from Japanese sources through club membership. The books usually carry approximately one hundred full colour pictures and are veritable treasure houses for tree shape reference, pots, accents, accessories, display detail and the feeling of the subject they impart. There are various alternative Japanese publications of the same type, some dealing in specialist material such as the Satsuki Azalea. There are of course other books containing pictures available and these may be ordered through libraries. They will not, however, be as rich in visual content.

## Colour slides
The 'Bonsai Clubs International' of America have done much to popularize visual programmes of varying types. There are slide and cine film programmes available to BCI members. In the United Kingdom club secretaries will often have access to slide collections of superior Japanese and native material.

## Collections
With careful study of the photographic material certain questions will arise. A great

number of the questions will actually stem from the two dimensional aspects of photography and these are best resolved by visiting a collection and literally walking round each tree and studying and absorbing the sculptural aspects of the Bonsai. It will make more sense if one is aware of the classical content of what one sees.

## Some basic classical criteria

### TRUNK
This is the core of the tree and conforms to the species and style of Bonsai portrayed. If deciduous, it is generally free of any conspicuous aberrations. The trunk should taper well; young trees are more or less equally columnar due to unrestrained growth and taper therefore, indicates age. The shape is a statement of the central theme of the design.

### ROOTAGE
This, unless the Bonsai is young, should be surfaced and displayed in as radial a fashion as possible. As a result of this formation two aspects are greatly and automatically strengthened: there will be a flared line like a bell-bottomed trouser-leg from the roots up into the trunk base; such roots will positively tie the trunk into the ground – thus becoming an integral part of the design – and can subtly echo the branch rhythm. There should be no hair roots apparent or crossing surfaced roots – both these suggest immaturity.

### BRANCHING
The branches are the means whereby the grower can echo both trunks and roots in terms of placement and design. They should obviously then be considered in terms of the mood of the tree and with due reference to the species. Deciduous subjects are convincing where the branches, whatever their form, ramify towards their tips and this transition works best if it occurs in three stages from trunk to periphery. Conifer branches are not usually dainty in the same sense but should, despite their greater weight, show a suitable diversity of form particularly where foliage is thinned to emphasize branch structures. Apical branches should be lighter.

### FOLIAGE, FLOWERS AND FRUIT
These must be healthy, of good colour and as neat in texture as possible. Flowers and fruit where present should be of suitable scale: a 60 cm (2 ft) Crab Apple for example in either flower or fruit should convey everyone's idea of the orchard tree in miniature. Careful selection of small featured trees contributes greatly to the quality of Bonsai.

### CONTAINER
This should subtly reinforce but not dominate the impact made by the tree. Proportionally, with slender trees, 20% pot to 80% tree is about right, while with heavier trees such as Pines, 40% pot to 60% tree will provide the necessary balance. Ovals and rectangles are the most versatile shapes and generally, the simpler the better, certainly until the tree has a very defined form when a change perhaps to a pot with some specific quality or detail might be considered. The colour of the container is most important with Bonsai of all ages: dull colours are *always* preferable but it is only with the less formal species, deciduous and fruiting subjects, that glazes may be freely used. Trees with ornate trunks may occasionally be displayed in pots that complement some specific characteristic of the design; cascade trees for example must be planted in pots that provide a firm visual base.

With these basic principles in mind, assess each tree in the collection and try to decide whether for you the design works or not. This is a test which it is only fair to apply to established Bonsai. Photographs taken at the time will be of use as a training aid to visual memory, particularly if notes are taken. With practice this process will perform the same function as a sketch book does to the painter; it is a means of sharpening awareness to critical pitch. If one feels able to make sketches of the salient points of a design the memory will be assisted further in that to sketch is to really penetrate – with a pencil one has to think, whereas a shutter just records. To really understand the success of the design it is necessary to discuss the styles so that one can bear the general principles in mind.

## STYLE DEFINITION

As mentioned earlier the Japanese design flair has led to the formation of recognized styles for shaping or training trees based on naturally occurring growth patterns. The various styles have been explored and recognizable nuances have developed.

### Formal Upright style

This is based on giant trees growing in isolation sometimes displaying outward signs of adverse conditions. The trees therefore can be gentle or heroic in feeling but they are always boldly stated with great emphasis on trunk quality. A tapered trunk makes for a convincing design.

Coniferous species used for formal upright Bonsai include: Pine, Yew, Spruce, Cryptomeria, Juniper, Cypress, Cedar and the deciduous conifers Larch, Dawn Redwood and Swamp Cypress. These will all be conical in form but there are proportional variants.

Deciduous species used for formal upright Bonsai include: Maple, Ginkgo, Elm, Zelkova, Beech, Hornbeam, Chestnut and occasionally Chinese Quince. The deciduous subjects are again broadly conical in form. Formal use is really confined to the Elm, Zelkova, Beech, Hornbeam, Chinese Quince and Ginkgo. The Ginkgo alone is broadly spear-shaped in profile with again many variants in shape. All the species except Ginkgo and Chinese Quince may be grown in the Broom style which can be considered a subclass of the Upright.

Coniferous Formal Upright Bonsai should display neat foliage; therefore texture size is important. Ideally the bark is rough and the trunk well shaped, with strongly defined branch and root lines. The classical form calls for a rather rigid branch arrangement radiating from the trunk so that segments of the foliage circumference occupy their position in an upward diminishing spiral. The branches

may be horizontal or raked downward but in either case conform to the theme.

From the base the first branch, either left or right, occurs at one third of the height, and the disposition is then as follows: second branch higher on the opposing side; third branch to the rear. This triad sequence is repeated but the sixth branch may be placed to the front if desired. Viewed from overhead and reading the branch disposition as a clock: No. 1 branch occurs at 9 o'clock; No. 2 at 3.30; No. 3 at 1.00; No. 4 at 8.00; No. 5 at 2.00 and No. 6 at 10.30.

It is not always possible to observe the literal classical disposition but the arrangement should at least strongly reflect the principles. The branches diminish in size and the vertical gaps between them also decrease near to the apex. Smaller branches above the initial six are less critically placed but must preserve the impression of a cone. Lower branches must be heavier and extra foliage weight is desirable.

Shapes of foliage contours should follow the theme throughout, most branches being based on a triangular plan section. Front elevations appear fairly flat. Other possible shapes are based on modified lozenge-shaped profiles. The secondary branches and foliage lines again echo the motif when viewed horizontally.

Rear branches give depth to the tree and those branches that angle slightly to the rear may be placed so that one is conscious of their shape offset from the broad front elevation. This apparent branch length difference contributes great charm to the tree. Those branches at the front of the design need to be of differing lengths for the same reason. There should never be any overlapping of foliage masses. With such broad, flat canopies, overlapped areas will suffer from lack of light and will weaken and eventually die.

Coniferous Formal Upright Bonsai, with trimming over years, develop a series of upturned twigs – these are in fact tertiary twigs rising from the secondary spread – which are gnarled, and add much strength to the form if glimpsed as upturned claws along branch lines. Pines particularly, which are subject to annual terminal replacement by pruning in August, develop gnarled branch ends as a result. These look superb if exposed here and there supporting the canopy of erect needles. The 'here and there' needs stressing – a Bonsai with overstated branches is as monotonous as the over-foliaged tree.

The trunk/branch junctions must be kept free of foliage. Old trees do not carry such inner growths and much of Bonsai is concerned with the illusion of age. The cleaning out of this foliage emphasizes branch weight so lower branches must be heavier. Again, if all junctions are exposed, the effect is monotonous, so here and there portions of trunk may be masked with the edges of secondary peripheries.

The apex must be well placed and shaped and not too big. If it is desirable to increase the apex dome it is better to allow neighbouring branches to contribute to the impression.

The roots provide the necessary anchor to the strongly tapered trunk. Their shape and articulation with the bole itself are therefore most important. Ideally the surface roots will flare from the bole in the manner of an Oak with soil-eroded roots. The forward facing roots should be shorter than those to the side and rear, suggesting perspective.

The most commonly seen Formal Upright has a spread of two-thirds of the height. Within this framework there are many variations in branch angles and frequencies, inspired in part by the species and in part by the mood of the tree. Older trees will often display fewer intact branches, their place being taken by vestigial silvered branch areas or Jin as they are known. Such trees have great appeal and their tenacious look reminds one immediately of storm veterans or the Bristle Cone Pines of the White Mountains.

Another variant currently popular is the Upright with a spread that matches or exceeds the height. The immediate impression is one of great power and branch lines are usually horizontal which reinforces the lateral quality. Pines and Yew are impressive in this variant and small-size Bonsai versions of Needle Juniper and Cryptomeria are also appealing.

## Formal Upright Deciduous style

This is sometimes seen as a formal tree in which case it follows the main lines already discussed, but, the branches in practically all cases will be in the raked downward manner which is a softer method of displaying the twigged secondary and tertiary lines. Individual branch lines may well show marked bowing which provides convincing support to the foliage canopy. Zelkova, Chinese Elm and Chinese Quince lend themselves to this treatment.

There is a relaxed form of the formal upright deciduous Bonsai which superficially resembles the Broom style. In this the trunk is not absolutely straight, the branches may have a less stringently disposed form and the species will have dictated the type of pattern encountered. Maple, Beech, Hornbeam, Birch and Chestnut look well treated in this way. In either style the root and trunk bole are as important as ever, with Zelkova and Trident Maple in particular often displaying a strong echo of the branch mass. When old enough, the bark colour continuing along each root adds a nice touch.

## Upright style Broom

This style is based on the natural growth patterns of Zelkova. It immediately evokes also images of the winter shape of Elms, Oaks, Beech, Birch and others.

In the major Broom style branch division begins at a point one-third of the way up a perfectly formed trunk; the branches spread out diffusely, dividing and sub-dividing into the finest of twigs. There should be no major conflict of lines created by limb crossing. The whole impression should be one of repose as the eye feeds on the wealth of branch detail in contrast to the simple shaft of the trunk. Proportional variants of the style are many and include: the intact leader type, where the branches surround and mound up around the trunk line like a busby; the very tall style, often with a flanking minor trunk that counterpoints the higher crown; the spreading, low style which is mushroom-like (latterly, Kyohime Maple is appearing more and more in this style); and the Broom Group, where the major tree (often good enough to stand alone) is surrounded by two or more nuclear clumps that continue and echo the form. The roots appear strongly formed and radial, and it is essential that these and the branches echo each other in the way they spring from the trunk.

In the Broom style great care is taken to avoid conspicuous trunk or branch aberrations; every portion should be rounded and unblemished and trees with scars are to be avoided.

## Informal Upright style

This style suits virtually all species, with the exception of those species best displayed formally such as Cypress, Ginkgo and Zelkova.

From the front, the trunk may feature several curves with the major axis shifting from the vertical by ten to fifteen degrees. The apex, no matter what the convolutions of form, should always be placed so that a plumb-line would establish the centre of gravity through the base, and the branches follow each outward thrust of the trunk, thus occupying a roughly triangular periphery. The negative areas between the branches should be clearly defined. From the side, the trunk angles backwards to a point at approximately half the height and then rakes forwards. This basic bowing posture contributes depth. The branches should be heavier – viewed as horizontal ellipses – in their bias to the rear of the design. A branch at the midway change of angle point extending some distance to the rear emphasizes perspective.

From the front or side the roots must be convincing and well defined. The 360° distribution is favoured with perhaps a little less forward weight.

The style is based on trees growing where conditions have caused some realignments in form, but of a gentle order. It achieves balance through carefully placed foliage masses that extend from the convex angles of the trunk. As with the Formal style, branches tend to be

arranged in triads with the first branch often being of some length, the tip thus defining the lowest point of the triangular periphery. The second branch and tip will be in an opposing direction and will describe the base of the triangle. The precise length and form of the first and second branches and their relationship to the apex thus establish the *form* of the tree. The shapes within the trunk should find their echoes in the branches, side branches and even the twigs thereby creating, together with the optical intervals or negative areas, the *rhythm* of the tree.

The trunk usually has one major curve that states the theme of the Bonsai. This may occur to the left or right of the trunk bole and is answered with a secondary curve in contra relation, the theme being repeated thereafter in diminishing curves. The secondary and subsequent curvatures occupy the upper two-thirds of the tree.

Branches strike out from the trunk at a downswept angle. An inferior Informal Maple for example, will often have branches that show an initial climb at this vital point. It is easily remedied by partially slitting the limb near the trunk (just score through the bark) and levering the offending portion downwards. Branches restate the form of the trunk and this usually means a series of curves. Abrupt angles should be included in the passage of each branch and these may be achieved by pruning above appropriately positioned buds. Any branch formed by totally similar means will be dull and great pains should be taken to ensure a combination of undulating and firmer lines. Branches display a major curve and progressively lesser movements, ramifying by thirds. Branch sections are generally triangular and tend to be domed when viewed horizontally.

## Slanting and Windswept styles

These both feature trunks with an inclination usually of at least thirty degrees. Both styles are based on trees growing in difficult environments. The Slanting is a gentle style with the angle of the tree balanced by carefully placed branching that leads the eye back to and beyond the centre of gravity thus stabilizing the design. The branches are shorter on the inner angle and longer on the outer. This makes for asymmetrical balance of the most satisfying type. Branches follow the triad formation and show diversity of length; branch sections are triangular and horizontal elevations may also be triangular or domed. The periphery is also broadly triangular and much richness can be added to the design by carefully monitored negative areas. The undersides of all the branches must be clean and it is possible for these to feature curved, straight horizontal, or downswept lines provided that the same motif is repeated and explored throughout.

The Windswept style is based on trees by the sea and in mountainous terrain that show the sculpting imposed by the prevailing wind. One side of the trunk is bare of branches in the major style, even featuring a dead, whitened section on the windward side, with the branches on the leeward side accentuating the trunk form. The Windswept is very definitely a 'mood' tree and does not rely on contrarelative thrust but rather succeeds as a strongly linear form (Cedar-like in a sense) in which every portion conveys the feeling of force.

Traditionally the Windswept style being abruptly one-sided and with the acute angle of the trunk, the lowest branch is long, the apex short and so a very obvious triangular form results. Proportional variants include: a very short trunk with an immensely long, lower branch and higher branches as abbreviated spurs, the total impact being that of a pennant; the rippled curved trunk, with the ripples repeated two or three times along branches, foliage appearing as isolated domed or triangular pads along the force line; and the low curved trunk capped with an umbrella-like head that puts one in mind of coastal areas. This low mushroom should still be offset away from the trunk to convey wind pressure.

Species used for Slanting and Windswept styles include: Larch, Pine, Juniper, Apple, Apricot, Azalea, Beech, Cotoneaster, Crab Apple, Elm, Hawthorn, Hornbeam, Maple and Quince.

## Semi-Cascade and Cascade styles

These evoke images from coastlines, mountains, quarries or even of understory plants. They have great force and feature respectively, a trunk curving outwards and down, sometimes to below the rim of the container, with an uptilted tip, so the whole appears to have a lazy 'S' configuration; and the second style, where the trunk again curving outwards, falls considerably below the baseline of the container, appearing as an elongated 'S', a straight or curved diagonal movement, or even as a vertical. The branches are treated as with the variants of the Informal style or more formally according to trunk form.

The Semi-Cascade appears as a squat edition of the Informal style with a greatly developed lower branch. The head (if present) of the tree is usually umbrella-like and centred above the pot. In reality, the head in this style, and that of the full cascade, is the first branch of the tree and the true head is the lowermost growing tip. The trunk should curve upwards and outwards, sometimes remaining as a straightish form with branches echoing and continuing the shape of the head, but more often the trunk will curve down and rise again with the branches appearing as repeats of the head. The straight trunk variant will quite often be a simple form with the foliage as a single contour placed above the trunk line for emphasis. The curved trunk variants look stronger where there are well-defined negative areas between leaf masses. Meticulous attention is paid to the cleaning of the undersides of all branch structures to lighten and emphasize the floating feeling of the tree.

The Cascade follows the same principles but, with the greater length of trunk, offers more variation in form. Variants include the classical vertical cascade, where the head occurs directly over the trunk bole and the trunk once over the rim, plummets down; in this the branches are trained to make firm horizontal movements often in diminishing size. The informal, where the trunk is curved in an 'S' or a series of bends and here the foliage masses are arranged on outer bends either in triads or in a nuclear arrangement of diminishing size echoing the head. Finally, there are multi-trunk versions of each. All informal cascades show an inswept branch that partially masks the edge of the pot. As the pots for semi- and full cascade are deep, in order to provide visual and practical balance, such line softening is a pleasant relief. Ideally, the roots should be evenly distributed with extra weight on the outer angle.

Both styles are planted in the centre of the pot and as such a placement calls attention to the roots and lower trunk, these must be forceful and simply stated.

## Literati style

These are trees which are based on or naturally resemble those depicted in the landscape paintings by the scholars of the Southern Chinese School.

This style is free form (in comparison with the others) but that does not mean undisciplined. Certain principles apply to Literati which are not found elsewhere and this is a pity. The trees should convey an elegant image. The branches are few and the foliage clusters abbreviated so that precise balance and form are maintained. A small container, usually round and with a rounded section is used. Without doubt the species best suited to Literati is the Pine, but, most species except the extremely formal may be successfully adapted.

## Driftwood style

These are trees from mountain ranges in the path of cyclonic winds and earthquakes. The trunks may be split, gouged out, spiralled or twisted and will have lost all but a tiny ribbon of live bark in the process. The exposed wood dries and bleaches in the sun and the combination of new foliage and white wood is not only beautiful but really evocative of age.

Driftwood dwarfed trees are carefully dug out and re-established. Training consists of developing complementary foliage masses around the existing trunk which is usually rigid and brittle and so immovable. As the trunks of natural Driftwood trees are so fantastic in form it follows that the foliage

masses will echo, augment or counterpoint the precise shape of each.

## Rock Grown style

There are two basic divisions of this style. In the first, the tree is placed astride the stone so the roots become a very strong feature, the success of the design often being decided by the pattern of the root structure in relation to the texture and shape of the stone almost irrespective of the tree itself. The trees of this style are found mostly in mountainous terrain usually where scree has subsided and left the tree in a location where it is perched on and clasping rocks.

The second variant is where the root mass is confined totally to the rock and the tree grows in a minute soil pocket. Here two main points should be observed: the tree, if big in relation to the stone will look well if the contour reflects that of the stone; if small, the tree or trees should similarly harmonize with the parent stone but must show neat foliage size. It is a question of scale which should be reinforced by following these principles.

All the styles considered so far are shaped single trunks but there are others classified by the manner of growth. The following are usually developed from a single plant, though they can also be formed as assembled trunk group variants.

## Twin Trunk style

This and the subsequent styles are reminiscent of trees on the skyline and quite often are umbrella shaped. The Twin Trunk looks better if the dominant trunk is taller and thicker in diameter. If the trunks are curved or slanted they will both observe the same direction. Trunks must blend well together and the trunk division should be as low as possible. Commonly, branch planes are treated identically through the planting with tiers projecting outwards. There should be no vertical conflict between the head of the minor trunk and overhanging major trunk foliage. No branch lines should cross and neither should there be any conflict of trunk or roots; the two entities blend but preserve their identity.

## Triple Trunk, Five or Seven Trunk and Clump

These all follow the principles of Twin Trunk but greater emphasis is placed on the height and thickness differences through the arrangement. Diagonal planting reinforces perspective.

## Raft style

This is a man-made group variant in which the trunk is laid over horizontally and the branches become 'trees'. One is a little conscious of the large central spine but nonetheless this naturalizes with time and if roots are surfaced this relieves the rather bulky base. Branches/trees in this and the Root Connected are styled entirely by Group principles.

## Root Connected style

This is the natural forerunner of the Raft. Wherever a freely suckering species is damaged (a classic example is the Elm) sprouts appear along major roots and the trunk base, and this phenomenon may be reproduced in miniature. The style may appear as having either a straight line base or a curving, snake-like form. In either style, the connecting areas, being in fact adapted branches, provide a lighter base than the Raft but one more consistently interesting than the roots of the standard group.

The following style is developed from several plants and all the multi-trunk styles just discussed may be developed by this means, with the exception of Raft and Root Connected.

## Group style

This is the style where there are many trunks arranged together creating the illusion of perspective in a very small space, in a manner recalling the principles of Palladian architecture.

All Groups depend for their effect upon the intervals between (negative areas) and the different relative thicknesses and heights of the trunks. If there is trunk movement, slanting or curved, every trunk should show the same general stance but with variation. Rear trunks are placed more closely for heightened perspective. No trunk should completely overlap viewed from front or side.

Foliage may be seen as a broad cap or dome or may closely follow the trunk arrangement and emphasize a nuclear grouping, with one or more heads at different heights.

It always follows that trunks on the right and left edges of a planting have their outer limbs encouraged by the removal of inner facing ones. Frontally placed central trunks should display lower trunks free of foliage and branches, while rear trunks may show dense low branches for increased depth.

Major trunks form the pivot around which the plan of the group evolves. There can be one, two or three of these. Groups normally comprise nine or more trees, so the major tree is planted to the front flanked on each side and slightly behind by two trees of slightly smaller dimensions. The major tree is planted at one third along the major axis of the container and at one third from either the left or right edge of the group. Other trees are added in order of importance and according to whether there are one or more dominant trees. There is always one dominant clump and other clumps must be clearly subsidiary in height and distinctly remote in location. In effect therefore one might be faced by one, two, or three triangular, carefully interrelated forms which will subtly echo the major planting. Straight trunk groups tend to be formally styled and the more relaxed forms tend to follow the informal style in branching.

Roots are as important in the Group as in the single trunk style. Furthermore the Group will appear more interesting if the different nuclei are planted at dissimilar ground levels. The major clump should be boldly stated. Practically all species are used in Groups.

These then, are the main styles. There are others, but one can learn to understand and appreciate Bonsai without reference to them. This far techniques discussed and suggested include: pictorial reference in various forms; photographic records; sketching; field study and the accepted standards of quality. The rest of this section is devoted to the practical techniques of Bonsai beginning with the development of the styles.

## STYLE DEVELOPMENT

All the recommended sources of material are discussed in later sections. The Japanese name for each style appears in parenthesis.

### Formal Upright style (Chokkan)

The trunk of the Upright Style Bonsai must feature a straight tapered trunk and this is acquired by the following means: natural material collected from the wild; layered tips of mature trees; nursery stock; cuttings; seed and grafts.

NATURAL MATERIAL

This is defined as a plant dwarfed at the time of collection (Fig. 1) by climatic and environmental factors or animal grazing. The most promising sites are in swamps, sandy areas, shallow soil pockets in mountainous areas, on scree and chalk hillsides. In the UK the natural material most likely to be found suited to this style occurs among Juniper, Yew and Pine species.

The tree should be around 45–60 cm ($1\frac{1}{2}$–2 ft) in height or be reduced to that if necessary, with good root flare and at least three or four well-placed lower branches. Without this basic sturdy frame it would not be worth collecting.

The tree is removed and established for at least two years in an acclimatization zone such as a cold greenhouse. It is potted in a temporary container large enough to house and encourage the root system without further pruning. Surface roots should be spread radially at this time.

The lower branches are formed first and this is best achieved by reducing new shoot activity in the upper reaches of the tree. Like

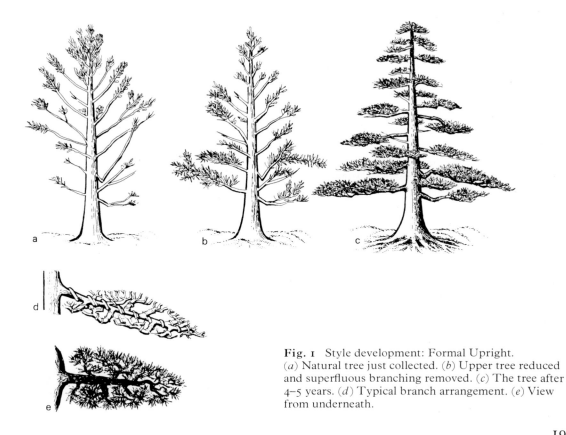

Fig. 1 Style development: Formal Upright.
(a) Natural tree just collected. (b) Upper tree reduced and superfluous branching removed. (c) The tree after 4–5 years. (d) Typical branch arrangement. (e) View from underneath.

pruning a privet hedge, this has the effect of channelling energy into the desired areas. The lower limbs swell and become heavy with the burden of the extra foliage thus encouraged. The heavier leaf mass enables one to build a dense cap above the visual support line of each limb and the additional underlying branch weight lends conviction to the design.

The triadic branch placement has been discussed and must be followed, at least in principle, for the proper appreciation of this style. Therefore, do remove superfluous branching at an early stage unless retained for extra thickening. Move gradually up the tree forming the Bonsai over a period of three–four seasons or more (by 'forming' I mean the slow emergence of branches in the right place). Do not worry about the head of the Bonsai until the tree is at least three-quarters formed. The head should be small in relation to the spread.

Branch lines should be kept clean underneath, any growths close in to the trunk or branch forks must be removed. Each limb must be adjusted to reflect the theme of the Upright, once chosen, and this means the branch angle, as the trunk is set in this style. The usual angle is horizontal or downswept. Each branch is wire-coiled and arranged with a corresponding angle. Sub-branches, which should be alternate, are wired sideways and the tips are elevated so the foliage when viewed as vertical elevations are seen as slow triangles or domes. In horizontal plan the branch peripheries appear as broadly triangular forms. Always maintain the broadly conical form of the tree.

Surfaced rootage is vital to this style and at transplanting time, usually about three years after collection, may be further encouraged by careful placement with the fingers of all existing basal roots. Careful consideration should be given to the form and regularity of these, any deficiency being corrected by top grafting in a seedling of the same species, grafting in a root section of the same species or by hormone stimulation. Hormone stimulation is simply the introduction of rooting powder through a hole drilled to the heartwood at ground level, the hole being covered by a heap of suitably light potting soil for the induced root to strike into – normally within a month or two.

LAYERING

This provides the best chance of obtaining tapered trunk and root flare for this style since the choice of trunk section is one's own and layering yields 360° of radial roots. By using this method of obtaining material the range of species suitable for this style is greatly increased and Cypress and Cryptomeria in particular, root very quickly.

Before establishment, even before separation, it is a good thing to remove redundant limbs to reduce the load on the new root system. After establishment the branches are built up from the base in the usual way but as foliage on layerings is usually dense, scissor work is necessary to establish planes and negative areas.

NURSERY STOCK

This offers diversity and the chance of finding a gem. It is quite usual, however, that the height of the tree will need to be reduced, so do not be put off if a possible, but tall, tree is found. The tree itself is 'read' from the foliage tip when complete so this enables one to convert the redundant trunk portion to good effect as a weathered tip or JIN. Sometimes portions of live branches and trunk may have areas of bark intentionally stripped away. These treated living areas are known as SHARI. Jin and Shari are illustrated in the picture sequences and fully discussed in the section on ageing. The Shari technique is normally carried out for thematic reasons and care should be taken not to abuse it, but it is a good method of disguising pruning wounds in the conversion of coniferous nursery stock.

CUTTINGS, SEEDLINGS AND GRAFTS

It takes longer to raise trees in this style, when they are propagated by these means, but they do have the advantage of offering maximum control over branch position and trunk form (Fig. 2).

The propagated trees are ready for training after they have become established and when

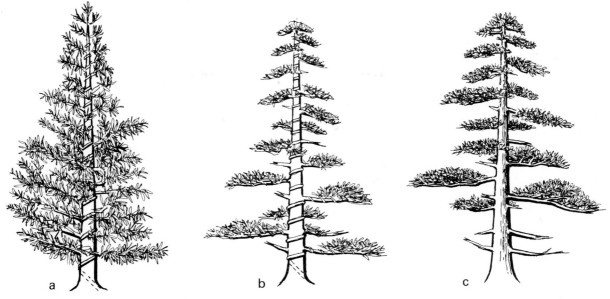

**Fig. 2** Style development: Formal Upright.
(*a*) Cutting after three years' growth, wire coiled for
straightness. (*b*) During year 4, main branches are
placed. (*c*) Year 5 sees the true form emerging.

they are woody enough to withstand having
their trunks wire-coiled in order to induce
straightness. This is usually at three years for
a seedling and possibly two for a cutting. The
objective in either case is the maintenance of a
vigorous, conically formed tree. Both should
be grown in broad, deep containers for sound
development. Feeding and trimming will produce dense growth and during year three all
superfluous branches are removed. At each
transplanting the roots must be arranged
radially.

During year four, the main branches should
be placed and angled with wire, and rough
contours established by means of frequent
trimming. By August of year four the side
branches may be arranged with wire and the
foliage refined and thinned with scissors.

During year five, the techniques of feeding
and pinching are followed with emphasis on
building the overall conical and individual
horizontal branch peripheries. The end of
year five will see a well-branched Bonsai
emerging.

It is also possible to raise Pines in this style
from grafts, if these are made right at the base
of the trunk. Two-year seedlings or cuttings
are used as understocks and these are beheaded short enough to accept a top graft that
literally occurs at root/trunk level. Such low
grafts are acceptable visually and give one the
chance to try a choice variety where only
limited material is available. Training techniques begin at the end of year two or
whenever the graft is well knit.

## Informal Upright (Tachiki)
The trunk of this style is gently curving with
two or more major convolutions. Foliage
should be well distributed round the trunk.
Such material is available from: natural material collected from the wild; nursery stock;
layerings; cuttings and seedlings; grafts and
divisions.

NATURAL MATERIAL
There is a wide range of species available in
the UK. Those commonly found include:
Scots Pine, Juniper, Beech, Birch, Hornbeam
and Willow. Likely sites for natural material
are as suggested for Upright Style Bonsai, and
disused quarries and abandoned railway lines

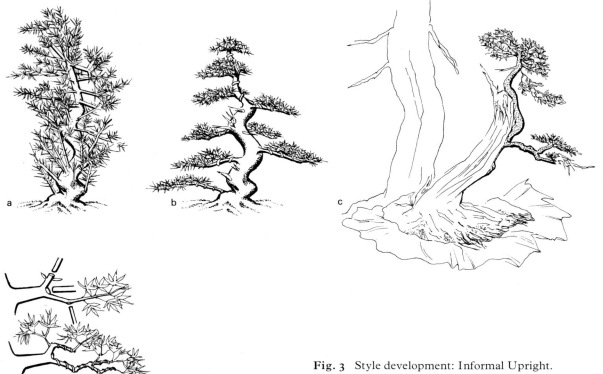

**Fig. 3** Style development: Informal Upright.
(*a*) Natural tree just collected. (*b*) Tree after 4–5 years' growth. Note where trunk was pruned for taper. (*c*) Tree by division. The one-sided root system is carefully wrapped. This technique enables one to split and collect really old-looking material. (*d*) Dome section branch development.

are also worth visiting. The trunk in this style appears to bow from the waist (Fig. 3). Viewed from the side the apex should lean forward from the baseline. This attitude is a vital element of the style and may be achieved through wiring, or by pruning, and the placement of the resulting spur. In such a case where the original leader is removed, the cut is made from the back and the new limb is raked forward and slowly built up like the branches.

The tree is planted in the usual way and pruning is carefully considered. Often very deep pruning at the apex and upper trunk is needed to restore visual balance. Branches alternate up the trunk, striking out from trunk convexities. The basic placement is again triadic and only one branch is allowed at any

growing point. Unless one is very lucky the trunk will be leggy or confused in line; equally, the branches will need sorting out so they emerge simply and strongly from the trunk.

Pruning should achieve four things: an overall conical form; lightening and simplification of the upper tree; reduction of all extraneous branch load; and grooming of every branch plane according to the chosen mode. Exceptions can be made where lower limbs are left for trunk thickening.

Dome section branch planes (Fig. 3*d*) are built up over three to four seasons. The apex is kept small and the first and second branches allowed a good spread. Bearing the basic conical form in mind, branches are allowed no

**Plate 1** Formal Upright Japanese Larch. 15 years from seed. Height 64 cm (2 ft 1½ in), spread 66 cm (2 ft 2⅜ in), trunk 5 cm (2 in). Unglazed grey rectangle.

**Plate 2** Same tree four hours later after grooming.

**Plate 3** Informal Upright Trident Maple. Approximately 30 years. Imported tree. Height 51 cm (1 ft 8⅜ in), spread 44 cm (1 ft 5½ in), trunk 7.5 cm (3 in). Unglazed grey rectangle. Front view. The tree has extraordinary taper and branches are triadically placed leaving trunk clear.

**Plate 4** (*above*) Rear view. Trunk line is masked.

**Plate 5** (*right*) Side view. Front faces right. Apex in forward placement gives depth.

**Plate 6** Root formation and buttress. Note the incredible regularity.

**Plate 7** Close-up explains root regularity: roots are in fact seedlings of Trident Maple that have been grafted on to produce a shallower root system, encourage flare and the table-top formation which will appear as the roots knit together by spreading sideways.

**Colour Plate 1.** Below: Formal Upright Scots Pine. 20 years.
**Colour Plate 2.** Right: Japanese Larch. Winter 1986/87.
**Colour Plate 3.** Bottom: This tree is the same as shown in Plates 1 and 20. Spring 1987.

**Colour Plate 4.** Right: Formal Upright Needle Juniper. 90 years.
**Colour Plate 5.** Below: Winter 1986/87.
**Colour Plate 6.** Below right: Winter 1986/87 branches removed.
Facing page
**Colour Plate 7.** Top: Informal Upright Scots Pine. 50 years.
**Colour Plate 8.** Centre right: Same tree. 40 years.
**Colour Plate 9.** Bottom left: Informal Scots Pine. 40 years.
**Colour Plate 10.** Bottom right: Same tree. 30 years.

**Colour Plate 11.** Right: Informal Upright style Scots Pine, Yatsubusa 'Beuvronensis'. 20 years.

**Colour Plate 12.** Below: Informal Upright Scots Pine. 66 years.

more than a two-inch extension per year and even this is arrived at through pruning back three or four times each season. Pruning is carried out with reference to bud position for desired angular changes and further growth extension permitted for ease of refinement with wire. No later than early August each year, branches are tipped back for the last time and any vertical shoots eliminated or pruned back drastically for sideways breaks of bud.

Each branch is wire-coiled and gently downswept with an uptilted tip. Every sub-branch is wired flat sideways and the tips elevated to reinforce the domed elevation; that is the principle, but in practice enough loose-ness is allowed to avoid uniformity. Branch lines are kept free of hanging foliage and negative areas maintained for the floating feeling of the style to succeed. Rootage is prominent in this style and is treated in the standard way.

NURSERY STOCK
This offers excellent scope (Fig. 4) and good foundation material exists among: Maple, Beech, Hornbeam, Hackberry, Elm, Birch, Crab Apple, Quince, Cotoneaster, Firethorn, Pine and Juniper. Container-grown stock is convenient both to transport and to study for potential. Points to look for are stout lower trunks with pleasing lines and lively lower

branches. Trunk taper is, as always, desirable. If there is an uninterestingly straight, higher trunk section, this may be pruned away from the back and the adjacent limb method used to create a new leader.

Unless one is very fortunate the branch system usually has to be built from scratch and this means removing everything except the skeletal triadic system. Only this basic stripping guarantees classical shaping. The method of raising is as for natural material.

LAYERING
In the UK, it is unusual to find branch tips on large trees that lend themselves but smaller shrubs can often yield large material. Coto-neasters and Firethorns are obvious exam-ples. If smaller material trunk sections are envisaged however, then the species listed under Nursery Stock, with the exception of Pine and sometimes Juniper, will all yield separable propagations inside one season. Material should be scissor shaped prior to removal.

CUTTINGS, SEEDLINGS, GRAFTS AND DIVISIONS
Cuttings, seedlings and grafts are all est-ablished and appropriately styled at the same stages as those for the Formal Upright.

Apart from the usual free-suckering species

Fig. 4 Style development: Informal Upright. (a) Nursery stock. Side view before pruning. (b) Side view after pruning. Adjacent limb will be raised to leader position. (c) Side view after some growth showing new trunk line. (d) Front view showing emerging tree with better taper.

such as Quince or Elm, examples can sometimes be found of rooted trunk divisions among such species as Juniper and Yew and these can be rapidly made up into imposing Bonsai. The technique is to dig out and carefully wrap the rooted section before division.

## Broom style (Hokidachi)

The trunk of this style is upright, based on the natural upturned broom appearance of the Japanese Zelkova. It has been adapted to other deciduous species, having broadly the same appearance, such as Elm, and certain Maple cultivars among others. It is rarely found in the dwarf natural state and is much prized when located, so these Bonsai are usually raised from: seedlings; cuttings; layering.

### SEEDLINGS

After germination, when the seedlings have produced one to two true sets of leaves, the seedlings are transplanted into a light and open soil mix. If man-made products are incorporated check they are guaranteed inert – seedlings will not tolerate any root burning. A radial root system is necessary to this style, so roots must be spread and evened with a very sharp sterile blade. This cutting of the roots aids ramification above and below the soil. The seedlings should be staked in the first and successive years to at least 25 cm (10 in) of their height and until they are past their tendency to sprawl. After four to six weeks a liquid feed should be given and repeated fortnightly.

The decision as to the favoured style of Broom (Fig. 5) is taken either in the first or second year depending on growth. Some seedlings will display tremendous vigour and these must be carefully watered and given good exposure to help regulate growth. If the tall single trunk variant or intact leader are preferred, then this treatment of sun and modest watering will encourage dwarfer trunk extension. The trick of retarding the growth by natural means also initiates taper without chopping the trunk, which becomes necessary when using other means of increasing its diameter. Zelkovas scar hugely and any redundancies need early bud removal. With the two variants mentioned, branches are programmed by bud retention and all others removed *before* they shoot. As always with Classical Bonsai, branches achieve form by tertiary ramification and so with vertical placement, where the lower branches begin at one third the total height or higher, initial intervals narrow until the diverse head is reached.

The classically formed Broom variant has the terminal checked by pinching at one-third the total height. The resultant buds are thin-

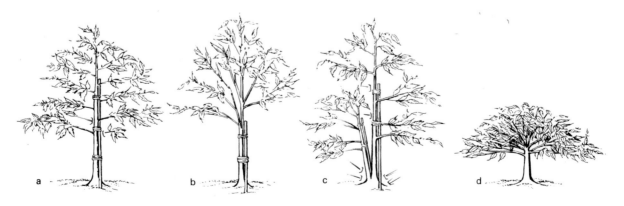

**Fig. 5** Style development: Broom.
(*a*) Intact leader variant. (*b*) Classic Broom. (*c*) Twin Trunk variant. (*d*) Low Broom variant.

ned and just the inner two retained so a 'V' is formed. Subsequent shoots are pinched back and thinned so a framework ensues that is varied but cleanly expressed. Avoid all crossing of main limbs and if necessary correct direction by light wiring, using covered wires. The negative areas between main branches and surrounding trunk/branch junctions should be well defined. The basic branch disposition of all Broom variants is the upturned umbrella.

The twin trunk Broom (Fig. 5c) may be initiated by early pinching of seedlings so that basal budding results. As soon as these are apparent, the embryonic trunk should be pruned to encourage strong base growth. Feeding is essential at this stage. A closely placed 'V' bud formation is chosen and all other buds removed. Almost from the beginning, one shoot will dominate. Allow the twin shoots about 10–12.5 cm (4–5 in) of growth and then put the plants on the sun and the modest water regime. As the dominant shoot elongates, let it bear more buds than the minor one. The foliage burden will increase the caliper difference between the two. Rub off inward-facing buds so the vertical negative area remains simply stated. The twin variant may additionally feature an intact leader or have the classically diverse trunk. The further care is as previously discussed.

The treatment of the low Broom (Fig. 5d) follows that for the classical variant with the exception of trunk height which is as low as 10 cm (4 in). Spread may be as much as three times the height. Training consists of apical suppression, systematically extended sideways over ensuing replacement terminals so a low crown is formed. Lower to middle branches are allowed free rein before checking. The result is a very appealing mushroom-like tree.

Broom groups are well worth the effort involved (Fig. 6). The placement is nuclear and a typical arrangement features: a very big tree; a secondary tree half its height and a tertiary tree one third the height of the major one. The major tree will be placed a little forward of centre and at one third left or right

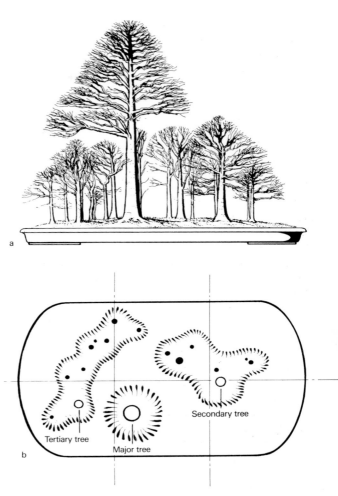

**Fig. 6** Style development: Broom: Broom Groups. Combination of the drawings and description of the Broom Group and the same from cuttings with the Group placement principles and drawings under Trident Maple Groups make this effect easily attainable.
(a) Winter form illustrating the main vertical and horizontal negative areas. Note the stabilizing effect of the plain areas on the flicker pattern of the twig traceries. (b) Plan view showing nuclear arrangement.

of the ground pattern. The secondary tree will be placed a little less than a third from the opposing side. The tertiary tree will occur at the halfway point between major tree and ground edge. The secondary tree attracts a grouping of subordinate trunks of lesser height and diameter and is remote from the major tree.

The major tree is bare-trunked to a height superior to the secondary group, thus avoiding visual conflict. Both major and secondary peripheries are fully and independently formed but echo each other. The tertiary tree and surrounding trunks of the third nucleus are the least stated vertical accents and the overall periphery often appears as a contiguous reinforcement of the major tree.

Trunk diameter and branch complexity remain constantly relative. Where extreme differences in diameter occur, the negative areas are vital to stabilize the fast visual speed – almost a flicker effect – created by the repeated verticals. Usually there is a substantial vertical negative area between the major tree and the edge of the secondary arrangement. Within the secondary arrangement, this negative area may be repeated once or twice on a slightly diminished scale. Within either subordinate group the minor negative areas may be decreased, thus contributing greater weight of trunk whilst of course preserving their individual slimness. This illusion and the variation it permits is the essence of the classic group.

CUTTINGS AND LAYERINGS

Cuttings provide the opportunity to raise choice clones of Zelkova, such as the red spring bud variety, and, together with layers, provide reliable means of obtaining uniform foliage for group work. The raising of Broom Bonsai from cuttings follows the seed method but obviates the waiting, and the insertion of cuttings of differing trunk diameter yields a crop already suited to training for groups.

For groups, rooted cuttings should be zoned into three sizes defined by height and thickness. The average Broom group will contain a dominant tree of 60 cm (2 ft) and approximately 3–4 cm (1–1½ in) in diameter. Secondary trees, in relation, will be 30 cm (1 ft) in height with a diameter of approximately 2.5 cm (1 in). Tertiary trees will be 20 cm (8 in).

Only the three key trees need this precise height and thickness of trunk, others should be raised to slightly under these proportions. In a typical group numbers are: major tree: 1; secondary tree: 1; adjacent trees: 5–7; tertiary tree: 1; adjacent trees: 3–5.

Bearing in mind that trunk diameter is largely increased by foliage weight, the main trees are developed to size. The major tree is given the intact-leader treatment, keeping the trunk free of branches and foliage to a little above the projected ceiling height of the secondary trees, that is to approximately 32 cm (13 in). Assuming one begins with 15 cm (6 in) cuttings for the major tree, one should aim for a slow height increase so that the major tree makes 60 cm (2 ft) in about five years.

The secondary tree is allowed an intact leader to three quarters the projected size of 30 cm (1 ft) so the trunk should be pinched out at 23 cm (9 in) and the apex encouraged to ramify. The annual growth rate of this and other material should conform to that of the major tree. Branching may begin at 7.5 cm (3 in). The tertiary tree is pinched out at half the projected height so this will occur at 10 cm (4 in). The tree is then slowly built up to the planned height using the classical Broom technique.

It is important that trees display uniform bark characteristics; therefore the tallest and thickest, and the smallest and slimmest, must all be of the same age. The differing sizes are achieved by: reduction or addition to leaf bulk which controls diameter (little trees are kept simple and big ones complex); development in temporary trays according to size, major tree in a 60 cm (2 ft) tray, secondary tree in a 45 cm (1½ ft) tray, tertiary tree in a 30 cm (12 in) tray and the subsidiary trees in 15 cm (6 in) trays.

All the trees are repotted regularly and the utmost attention is paid to preparing the root mass for group assembly. At the last two repottings prior to assembly, the subsidiary tree should be lightly root pruned and the larger trees more firmly dealt with than usual. Over the ensuing seasons the tidier root mass of the larger trees and the larger root mass of the minor trees achieve some sort of balance.

This is followed in principle at subsequent group repotting where dominant areas are always lightened to strengthen the smaller trees.

LAYERING

Often an ideal Broom section is discovered on some plant and layering is the obvious way of securing the precise piece. The subject may be shaped and refined before attempting layering. Trunk sections of about 2.5 cm (1 in) are the most aesthetically rewarding and practically manageable thicknesses for potential Broom. After establishment, training is standard.

Whichever method is employed to raise the Broom it should be borne in mind, where plants of Zelkova and Chinese Elm are concerned, that structuring and raising as discussed takes place against a background of constant soft pruning; it is the key to success with these plants.

## Slanting style (Shakan)

The trunk is inclined at an angle of thirty degrees and needs taper to balance the rather open frame. The best subjects are available through: natural material; nursery stock; and by layering.

NATURAL MATERIAL

In the UK the most commonly found Slanting style occur among Hawthorn, Juniper, Larch, Pine, Beech and Elm.

On establishment, determine the strongest visual combination of trunk and root line and relate existing and/or projected branch lines to these (Fig. 7).

Major surface roots should be felt for around the trunk and the soil brushed away. When the main root buttresses are all exposed to a third of their depth, the trunk bole can be fully appreciated and any defective rootage corrected by hormone stimulation. The trunk angle is the paramount factor, with the bole as the core, so if necessary correct the rootage artificially as suggested. Natural trees seldom display their best surface roots where one would choose.

Branch arrangement is usually in straight or downswept curved lines, shorter on the inner angle and longer on the outer. Stability may be achieved quite simply by ensuring the first outer angle branch rakes back across the root bole. Successive outer angle branches are similarly raked and diminish in size quite abruptly, so preserving a narrow line from base to apex. Inner angle branches are less raked but shorter, their tips often forming an almost vertical line beneath the apex.

Foliage planes look best as defined horizontal steps with wide negative areas between. A triadic placement simplifies matters when one is faced with either a multiplicity of trainable limbs or a complete design project with new shoots. Foliage planes may be triangular both in plan and section or dome sectioned with either a flat or concave base.

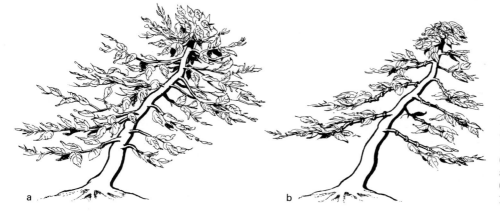

Fig. 7 Style development: Slanting. (a) Natural tree just after collection. (b) The tree after 3–4 years' growth.

**Fig. 8** Style development: Windswept.
(*a*) Natural tree just after collection. (*b*) The tree after 3–4 years' growth. (*c*) Same tree developed as the 'long, low branch' variant. (*d*) Low windswept variant. (*e*) Rippled curve variant.

In the year after establishment the main limbs are pruned back on the outer and encouraged on the inner angle and main directions achieved by wiring. Suspended wiring is the best method for main placement. Some very gentle rudimentary placement of the foliage planes (to assist the eye when pruning) may be attempted if the suspended method is used.

During year two, more detailed wiring may take place provided the bud activity is obvious and vigorous over the whole plant. Should this not be apparent, delay further training for another year.

NURSERY STOCK
This method gives one the opportunity to develop additional species such as Crab Apple, Apricot, Quince, Azalea, Cotoneaster and Wisteria. Once again one looks for trunk taper and promising roots. Branches usually have to be removed and totally restarted. Total removal is not practised on Pines.

LAYERING
Good Slanting Bonsai can often be developed from redundant tip material on other Bonsai, nursery stock or the garden shrubbery. The great advantage of this style is that straight trunk areas, usually boring, can be freely adapted.

## Windswept style (Fukinagashi)
The trunk is inclined usually at an angle of thirty degrees or more. The best material comes from natural material and nursery stock.

NATURAL MATERIAL AND NURSERY STOCK
Despite prevailing winds sculpting larger trees, the climate in the UK is too mild to produce many dwarfs in this style. Material of appropriate size does exist however and is usually best looked for on moors and swamps. More typically, Windswept Bonsai (Fig. 8) in this country are found as the result of over-

crowding and light restriction and as such are on the spindly side. Their re-establishment therefore takes longer than most and should be followed by a good feeding programme.

After establishment, vestigial limbs on both sides of the trunk should be bark stripped in preparation for Jin. If the wood is still fresh it may be wired into shape and position and even the trunk may feature a whitened Sharimiki section on the windward side. The decision as to whether or not to peel the bark can only be taken when every aspect of the potential design has been considered and here, notes and photographs come to one's assistance.

The precise angle of the trunk is all-important and determines the entire design. If the long low branch is decided on, the apex and higher limbs should be allowed tentative growth and every bud encouraged on the low one. Foliage sections follow those for the Slanting style.

The low variant (Fig. 8d) is developed in the same way but with extra emphasis on the lower limb and the brevity and simplicity of the apex and higher areas. The rippled-curved variant (Fig. 8e) can be developed from weedy material by wiring or by using naturally curved trunks as a foundation. The general trunk axis in this variant is low with the apex almost on a level with the roots. The trunk displays marked 'S' bends, up to five of them in diminishing size.

Foliage is arranged to appear on the tops of the outer bends and lower emphasis is provided by continuing the foliage lines downward and from branches coming from the convexities of the alternate inner bends beneath. These lower lines curve gently towards the low apex. The effect is that of frozen photographic action. The design has an explosive quality when properly executed.

The foliage tips and twigs of all variants display a marked angling toward the leeward side. Apart from the rippled curved variant, other variants of the style display simple, almost stiff branch lines.

## Semi-Cascade style (Han-Kengai)

In this style the trunk is usually strong, squat and abruptly tapered. Likely material is available through: natural material; nursery stock; cuttings and by layering.

NATURAL MATERIAL

In the UK, Pine, Juniper, Hawthorn and Yew are the most available species largely because of their extreme adaptability to differing adverse environments.

Only trees which are flattish or have a long low branch are chosen. Establishment is carried out in deepish containers so initial training is aided by this likeness to the final container. One decides first whether the tree is to feature a head situated above the root bole or if not, where to place the emphasis of the form, the decision here being aided by the nature of the material.

STRAIGHT TRUNK VARIANT

Trees that are suitable for this variant are low and sturdy with a simple, straight, or a *slightly* curving trunk (Fig. 9a–b). The lower trunk is free of foliage which occurs as a simple cap occupying about two thirds of the terminal end of the tree. Trunk angle is so extreme as to be almost horizontal. Trees should have good branching at least half way along the trunk. Trunk angle must first be established, at repotting time or by temporarily jacking up one end of the container, before training begins. Branch training then consists of a simple triadic placement with emphasis on radial disposition. Foliage profiles are mounded domes and these may be flat, convex or concave-based provided the theme is constant. Detailed wiring must ensure every foliage plane is as widely spread as possible to reinforce the simple visual impact of trunk shaft and head. If the trunk line is very severe with the cap sitting above it, bring a minor branch forward and down and repeat the main head form in miniature. This simple repeat motif is very effective.

CURVED TRUNK VARIANT

Trees suited to this variant (Fig. 9c) can be short and sturdy, or slender but in either case lower branches are necessary. The trunk

a

b

c

d

e

features a head that dominates the root bole. The height of the head and the shape of the supporting trunk are the first considerations and normally they constitute one third of the visual mass.

Trunk angle is extremely shallow and the trunk just clears the pot rim before curving away downwards. When and where the trunk rises again the design can be greatly strengthened if this third movement parallels the first trunk angle at the bole. The essential form is then like a relaxed lightning flash. Extensions of the third movement may follow the first angle or be contra-relative and branch training may begin when the form of the trunk section supporting the new apex over the root bole has been decided. A gentle 'S' usually works well at this point.

Branch disposition around this new trunk is triadic and extension is planned so emerging lines will equal or extend beyond the line of the pot. The entire tree gains force if there is a simply stated change of plane in foliage mass between the new head and the downswept lower limb. This is further strengthened if a distinct negative area is preserved between the two. Often, the foliage base of the head will parallel the first angle and almost sweep the

**Fig. 9** Style development: Semi-cascade: Trunk development.
(*a*) Straight line variant. (*b*) Straight line variant where severity is softened by the repeat motif of the lower branch. (*c*) Curved trunk variant. Note the contra-relative relationship of head and lower mass. The trunk form is the relaxed lightning flash. (*d*) Nursery stock. Heavily pruned Satsuki Azalea. (*e*) Same tree after 2–3 years' growth.

pot rim, whilst the lower foliage cap flows away from this angle.

The lower limb must have branches that are sympathetic to the shapes already created. These may appear as single shallow domes supported along the limb with visual gaps beneath, or as widely remote pads that follow the basic plane but always remain subordinate to the main frame. It is easy in this, and the Cascade style, to introduce too much detail and fragment the overall profile. Even foliage caps need stringent grooming and more than the usual care in cleaning of underplanes.

NURSERY STOCK
The choice of suitable species is broad and includes Maple, Crab Apple, Quince, Cotoneaster, Wisteria, Sophora, Laburnum, Willow and Satsuki Azalea.

Again, flattish subjects are usually the best (Fig. 9d–e) but keep an eye open for any trees with a strong lower limb that can be adapted. If additional curving is needed and the lower limb is more than thumb thick, it is better to look for a side branch along the limb that can act as a replacement spur. The limb is then pruned to the convenient side branch and this is wired to the desired form. Such major surgery on a deciduous subject takes place out of sight at the back of the limb but evergreens often may have the wound converted to a Jin. The vertical main trunk is either adapted to the design by shortening and training, or is converted to Jin, or removed completely. The method, after establishment or repotting is as for natural material.

LAYERING
This can be 'instant'. Cotoneasters commonly raised by layering often merely need pruning to be basically successful. Look for arching material.

CUTTINGS
This is the slower way but Wisteria for example and Willow can readily be rooted and make splendid subjects. Both species respond well to pinching and spur pruning. Use deep pots.

## Cascade style (Kengai)
In this style the trunk is usually short and squat and the branches long. Material is available through: natural material; nursery stock and by layering.

NATURAL MATERIAL
Practically any species *may* be found but in this country those that appear most natural when trained are Pine, Juniper and Yew (Fig. 10). With Pines, the material will often be found just poking above heather with almost basal side branches, that snake along below the stems of the heather, or, it may be a bigger, partially dwarfed tree with old bark, yet still retaining the basal branches under the heather. Juniper and Yew, which in this country do not occur in anything like the same num-

bers, are mostly animal grazed and so are flat and spreading.

Pine and Yew are relatively flexible when old but Junipers can be very brittle, so, even though the Cascade is rather an extreme style, it must be tempered more than usual by respect for the form of the collected material. Material is again established in deep pots.

FULL FORMAL CASCADE
This curves economically over the pot rim and plummets down with the tip below the base of the pot. There are straight and curved variants.

CURVED VARIANT
The curved trunk features a series of diminishing curves with branches triadically placed along its convexities; in fact, it greatly resembles an inverted Informal Upright in disposition. It is traditional to bring a branch or branches across to soften and mask the pot line. This minor touch certainly integrates the two elements.

Material should have at least one basal branch to form the head over the root bole. This is a must in the formal Cascade. In working with old and intractable material it is often safer to utilize existing trunk features and prune back on the replacement leader basis than to risk spoiling the tree by imposing drastic realignments, or, reserve material for the straight line variant.

If the trunk is malleable, wire it and bend at the chosen branch points, remembering to leave each branch on the convex side. The bends should be three-dimensional; simply follow the Informal Upright. Such wiring is tiring to the tree, so beyond rudimentary placement with suspended wires, delay detailed work on the foliage to year two.

During year two foliage planes may be arranged, if buds are prominent, and the tree is flourishing. Use a generally downswept theme. Domed profiles are pleasing and look especially good with a concave base. The planes in the head over the root bole follow the theme and usually lead into the form rather than away from it. An interesting and pleasant

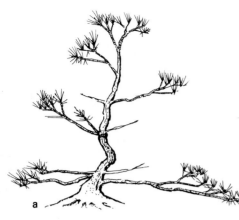

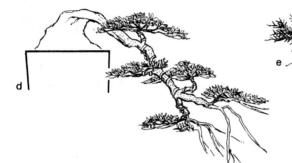

**Fig. 10** Style development: Cascade.
(*a*) Natural tree, Scots Pine, just after collection.
(*b*) Same tree after 4–5 years' growth trained into the curved variant. (*c*) Natural tree, Yew, just after collection. (*d*) Same tree after 4–5 years' growth trained into a Formal Cascade. (*e*) Natural tree, Juniper, just after collection. (*f*) Same tree after 6–7 years' growth trained as Full Formal Cascade straight line variant.

effect can be achieved by breaking the planes into related subplanes.

STRAIGHT VARIANT

This plunges vertically downwards and features a formal head and branches that flow outwards in steps. Very stiff looking material can be successfully trained in this style. The formal foliage placement justifies and softens the severe lines. Training is relatively easy and beginning with the head which is trained first, the chosen motif is repeated at decreas-

ing intervals down the trunk, usually on a triadic basis. The head is the emphatic area and as such should be well spread and dense. The negative areas immediately below the trunk bole arch, and above the first descending branch, are critical, as all negative areas relate to these in size and shape.

If the main descending spine is visually flimsy, additional side shoots can be wired down to strengthen the vertical and contribute additional three dimensional foliage spread. Be careful not to create too much

34

**Plate 8** (*above*)   Slanting style Scots Pine.
Photographed in 1978, compare with line drawings
and Colour Plate 17.

**Plate 9** (*above right*)   Semi Cascade in the making:
Scots Pine. In the first year of training after collection.
Height 69 cm (2 ft 3½ in), spread 67 cm (2 ft 2¾ in), trunk
4.5 cm (1¾ in).

**Plate 10**   Cascade style Chinese Juniper.
Approximately 40 years. Unglazed grey rectangle.
Discussed in Design Assessment.

**Plate 11**  Cascade style Scots Pine. Approximately 30 years. Collected tree. Height 68 cm (2 ft 3 in) spread 85 cm (2 ft 10 in) trunk 7 cm (2¾ in).

**Plate 12** (*below left*)  Root over stone style Mountain Maple. Approximately 30 years. Imported tree. Height 68 cm (2 ft 3 in), spread 85 cm (2 ft 10 in), trunk 7 cm (2¾ in). Medium stone variant.

**Plate 13** (*below*)  Group style Mountain Maple. 10 years from cuttings. Unglazed brown oval. Just assembled, the work of linear simplification now begins.

36

**Plate 14** Twin trunk style Japanese Larch. 10 years from seed. Height 34 cm (1 ft 1½ in), spread 40 cm (1 ft 4 in), trunk 5 cm (2 in). Unglazed brown rectangle.

**Plate 15** Five trunk style Mugo Pine. 10 years from seed. Height 31 cm (1 ft ⅜ in), spread 50 cm (1 ft 8 in). Ceramic dish planter.

**Plate 16** Cluster style in the making Scots Pine. First year of training. Unglazed brown oval.

visual flicker when the verticals are placed together and be content with rudimentary positioning. Again, if bud development is weak during the year, delay refinement until vigour is apparent, because detailed wiring is extensive in this style. Because this style is so ornate every shoot must obey the profile, any untidiness tipping the balance into total chaos. If in doubt, place the tree against a plain background and walk back far enough to see mass instead of detail. Conflict usually occurs where negative areas are small and many. Simplify by pruning or wiring foliage into broader, slower passages.

In both Semi and Cascade styles the design is greatly strengthened if the root is a strong feature so follow all the standard techniques. Remember the cleaning of foliage under-planes as this reinforces the suspended feeling of both styles.

NURSERY STOCK AND LAYERING
Both follow the principles outlined above but feature the more exotic species, such as Maple, Apple, Quince, Cotoneaster, Wisteria, Sophora, Laburnum, Willow and Azalea, which often appear more convincing

**Fig. 11** Style development: Literati.
(a) Natural tree, Scots Pine, just after collection.
(b) Same tree after 6–7 years' growth. (c) *upper* The stork's leg as a spatial recreation; *lower* Stork's leg motif as the brush-drawn element. (d) Cuttings after 3–4 years' growth. Satsuki Azalea.

than the natural item, which can look surprisingly artificial. Beech for example are often found as Cascade but look contrived. Use deep pots.

## Literati style (Bunjin)
Literati Bonsai are thin-trunked but full of character and the best material is available through natural material and cuttings.

NATURAL MATERIAL
The most likely and best species in the UK are Pines and Junipers. Of these, Pines (Fig. 11a–b) are probably more widely available, those from sandy moorland sites being particularly suited as such conditions (deep heather and dry soil) create overshading and drought. This causes the trunk to realign many times as leading shoots are damaged and low branches, if alive, are so weedy that their removal leaves the trunk unscarred. Such trees, crooked and curved, though dimensionally frail, give an impression of strength. The bark is often well developed, such trees – in the south at any rate – being commonly thirty to fifty years old. Needle growth is sparse and confined to apical zones but this also is advantageous in the formation of Literati.

To understand why all these negative characteristics create a positive, in Bonsai terms, it is necessary to go back to the origins of the style: the brush-drawn landscapes of the Confucian scholars, who were called Bunjin. It is the calligraphic qualities, a

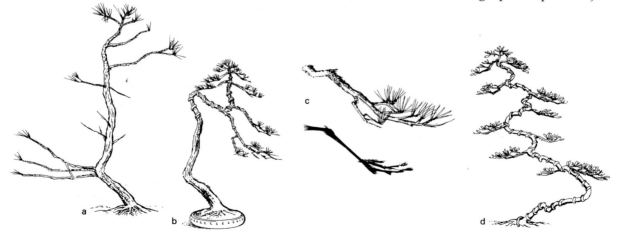

technique literally more akin to writing than painting, that created the elegant abbreviated tree forms in the pictures.

Appropriately, two elements from brush drawing are the key to the training of Literati: the form should be spontaneous and charged with energy and the branch arrangement, said in painting to be like a stork's leg, looks superb when spatially recreated for this style (Fig. 11c). There is no typical Literati tree but countless variants that respect the principle of a ribbon trunk connecting the compact head and circle of the pot. Elements it *is* possible to tie down are the stork's leg arrangement of the branches (for which see the diagram) and the size of the pot, which is normally no bigger than any one of the foliage planes! When successful, the Literati has a kite-like, floating quality.

CUTTINGS
These present ample scope for the creation of something really free. Currently, Satsuki Azalea (Fig. 11d) is appearing more and more in this style in Japan. Cuttings of Satsuki are grown tall and then curved in a contra-relative fashion recalling the Informal style but in a very understated way. The curves are repeated several times up the trunk. Some sixteen to seventeen curves in a trunk 60 cm (2 ft) tall are common. The curves described are minor and the trunk is now given two or three general directions or larger curves and then the tree is rested for a year. During this year many buds will appear on the trunk and those occurring on the newly created outer bends are retained but all others are rubbed off.

During year two the new shoots are encouraged by feeding and sun exposure. They are pinched to keep them compact and arranged with covered wire in downswept curves. Detailed wiring as always, comes later. The aim in a Literati with a continual branch pattern up the trunk, is always to preserve a narrowly conical periphery, so attention is paid to constant pinching.

As foliage becomes more dense, consider the relation between negative area and leaf mass. One should dominate, otherwise there is fussiness instead of elegance. All Literati need constant grooming so that not one untidy leaf or extraneous element remains. With Azaleas, underplanes need cleansing very often. Foliage profiles may be domed or triangular and bases may be flat, concave or convex in careful relation to the degree of branch curvature.

## Driftwood style (Sharimiki)

This is actually developed around the shapes of the dead, bleached trunk areas, so the form may follow any style and the style feature any species. Pines and Junipers are the most common. Natural trees are the most dramatic but damaged or faulty Bonsai can often be successfully converted to this style.

NATURAL MATERIAL
In the UK the climate is too mild for the Driftwood style to be commonplace. They do however exist and not always in high country; sheep and deer are great creators of Driftwood Bonsai and the results occur from the Hebrides to the South Downs. Rock falls also damage trees, causing trunk splitting and gouging. Check areas of loose scree in the mountains and look too, for pockets of soil in rocky terrain – both these often house something choice. This all sounds very distorted but trees with Sharimiki and Jin look very natural. The silvering of the dead portion mellows the impression and new growth looks very rich against it. The roots are often very poor and such trees need very careful establishment. No shaping should be attempted until the tree has enjoyed two or three seasons of vigorous growth. The freely expanding foliage means the roots are following suit and training usually only follows existing growth points by bulking and extension. Another technique is that of grafting in new branches at chosen points. This is successful where the supporting live section is plump and smooth; where the live section is scrawny and the bark rough, however, grafting is technically far more difficult, though not impossible.

Newly collected Driftwood trees require establishment aids such as some form of soil-

The Art of Bonsai

heating cable, Vitamin B$_1$ transplant solution, and some type of humidity retention device like a mist unit or polythene tent. A cool greenhouse provides an ideal establishment area.

At this point, I really could not do better than quote my brother-in-law, Ian Price, after a collecting trip in the Tehachapi area in America:

'A most satisfactory experience, yielding six trees, mostly in the four- to six-inch Driftwood trunk category and from two to four foot in height. The trick is to pull apart the oldest clumps of Juniper, which fall outwards and layer the individual trunks – thus yielding single trunked trees. So far they all look good, with new growth and roots, after four weeks. In the mountains they were sprayed with a chemical to help prevent loss of moisture over the whole top, had sphagnum, followed by black plastic, wrapped round their roots and were soaked for twenty-four hours in Vitamin B$_1$. The cut root ends were daubed with a rooting hormone and then sprayed with a systemic fungicide.'

The wait during the establishment period does give the chance to study the tree and get some idea of how to improve the form. One solution is to photograph the tree in black and white and then lay transparent film over the print so designs can be visualized by drawing future growth patterns in wax pencil or water soluble marker pen. Visual retention is a great help here, but in the meantime, textbooks, pictures, photographs and trained Bonsai should be studied for any reference to parallel training problems. Driftwood Bonsai have obvious abstract impact and often the form is really non-classifiable. Guide lines for one of the most awkward are:

FORM
Short, multi-leadered, spiky Jin everywhere.

TRUNKS
Choose one that is well placed and can dominate (Fig. 12). If living multi-trunks are planned, select number and purge others of foliage. Establish position that shows living trunks to equal advantage – a diagonal axis reinforces perspective.

The major trunk needs to reach 45 cm (1½ ft), the secondary trunk, 22.5 cm (9 in), the tertiary trunk, 15 cm (6 in) and so on. The major trunk looks well at one end or at a point one-third along the arrangement.

Grow the major trunk on and make sure it continues the theme of the base, whether straightish or curved. This is achieved by wiring. Once set, arranged and softened in line, the limb has the wire removed and is grown on, sometimes to three or four feet or more. The ensuing thickness soon blends the new line into the old. The trunk is then pruned back hard to size and the side shoots are arranged for development into abbreviated, radially disposed layers.

Normally, the tertiary and secondary trunks are developed first and the major trunk is kept pinched back to encourage these, but, as the major trunk is at this point only marginally major, keep a watchful eye on it for weakness. As others start to sprout and grow away, allow them a 60 cm (2 ft) extension before pruning back. This strengthens the emerging trunks and produces great side shoot activity. Rudimentary wire shaping of smaller trunks can take place after extension if the increase in diameter contemplated is no more than 1.25 cm (½ in) total, otherwise it must take place before to avoid damage.

Foliage profiles look well as domed layers. The foliage masses on the secondary and tertiary trunks may be considered as one and kept distinct and subordinate to the major trunk. The overall mass looks well divided like this and finer placements follow Group principles. In outline, the minor periphery is long and a repeat of the major, but about a third of the width.

There should be clearly defined vertical negative areas separating the periphery of the secondary and tertiary cluster from the periphery of the major trunk. The major trunk foliage will overhang the minor trunks slightly so this gap is vital. If the overall height of the Group is 45 cm (1½ ft) or so, the initial root to

40

**Colour Plate 13.** Left: Informal Upright Satsuki Azalea. 15 years.
**Colour Plate 14.** Below: Close-up of Satsuki Azalea.

**Colour Plate 15.** Left: Twin Trunk style Satsuki Azalea. 15 years.
**Colour Plate 16.** Above: Close-up of Satsuki Azalea.

**Colour Plate 17.** Above: Informal Upright Dunkeld Larch. 28 years.

**Colour Plate 18.** Above right: Informal Upright Red Maple 'Seigen'. 90 years.

**Colour Plate 19.** Right: Spring 1987.

Facing page

**Colour Plate 20.** Top Left: Informal Upright Trident Maple. 80 years.

**Colour Plate 21.** Bottom: Spring 1987.

**Colour Plate 22.** Top right: Informal Upright Crab Apple. 30 years. Spring 1987.

**Colour Plate 23.** Top: Broom style Chinese Elm.
12 years. 1979.
**Colour Plate 24.** Top left: Spring 1985.
**Colour Plate 25.** Above: Winter 1986/87.
**Colour Plate 26.** Left: Driftwood style Pyracantha.
80 years.

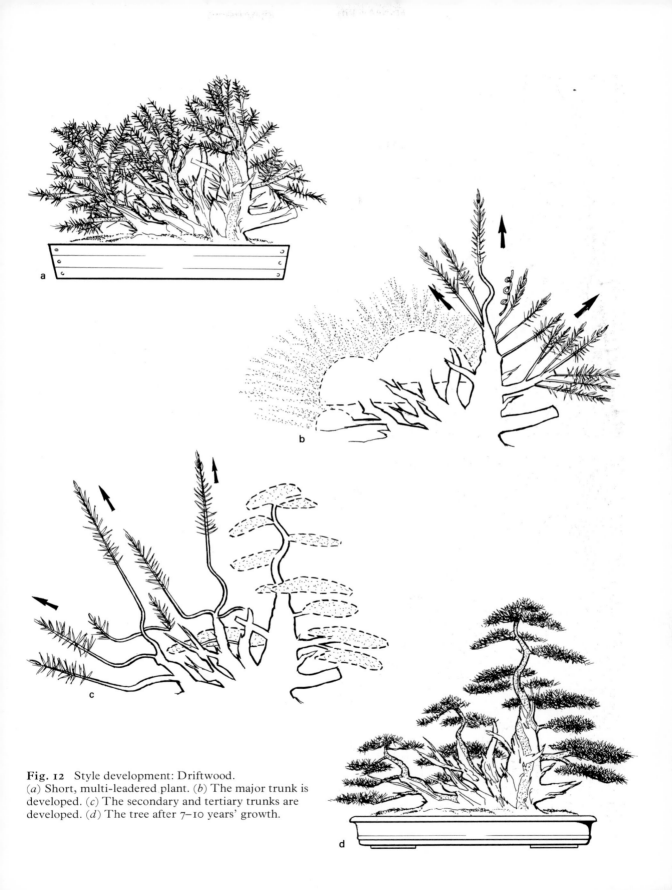

**Fig. 12** Style development: Driftwood.
(*a*) Short, multi-leadered plant. (*b*) The major trunk is developed. (*c*) The secondary and tertiary trunks are developed. (*d*) The tree after 7–10 years' growth.

The Art of Bonsai

branch negative areas should be about 7.5 cm (3 in) at the major trunk, 2.5 cm (3 in) at the secondary and possibly less at the tertiary. Subsequent gaps are closer but the odd major gap is effective. Underplanes are cleaned and secondary branch structures kept open at the base to emphasize form.

As the foliage mass develops the Jin can be better assessed. The front elevation of any Driftwood Bonsai needs the background stability provided by foliage or open space. If instead there is visual conflict, remove or shorten the offending portions and preserve those at the side of the arrangement.

Surface roots are important to tie the complex mass firmly into the soil. Try to arrange them radially but group them for simplicity. A medium shallow rectangle or oval pot is suitable.

Those Driftwood trees with more identifiable trunks are best trained in the manner of the styles they suggest. However, by far the greatest percentage of Driftwood trees are very abstract and this quality has contributed the most exciting visual images in Bonsai. An example of the development of a Driftwood tree will be found in the section on 'Evolution in design' in Chapter 4.

**Root Over Stone style (Sekijoju)**
Trunks in this style are usually compact and tapered but there are proportional variants. The best material comes from cuttings. Recommended species for this style are:

Azalea, Cotoneaster, Cypress, Jasmine, Pine, Quince, Juniper, Yew and Maple.

The basic technique is simple and consists of arranging the tree firmly astride a depression in the stone and conducting the roots down fissures to the soil, but it is so important to form a harmonious unit that the following section is divided into two parts: Applications and Methods.

*Applications*
Variants include the medium tree over a medium to tall stone; tall tree or trees over a low stone; and sometimes even a group may be grown astride a stone (Fig. 13).

MEDIUM TREES
The usual medium-sized tree is trained into what may be almost classified as a Cascade tree. It features at least one low branch and this really establishes the mood of the Bonsai. The low branch may be a simple arc in which case the tree is then largely a 'theme and variation' on this, or the branch may be gnarled and again, echoed throughout the rest of the tree.

The trunk form can be an abbreviated Informal shape (Fig. 14), usually a single 'S'. The low branch springs from the first outward trunk curve and this may be very low indeed, depending in part on the angle of articulation between trunk and stone (this in turn being determined by the degree of trunk curvature) and in part by the planting angle of the whole

**Fig. 13** Style development: Root over stone. (*a*) Medium tree over medium stone. (*b*) Medium trees over tall stone. (*c*) Tall tree over low stone. (*d*) Group over stone.

42

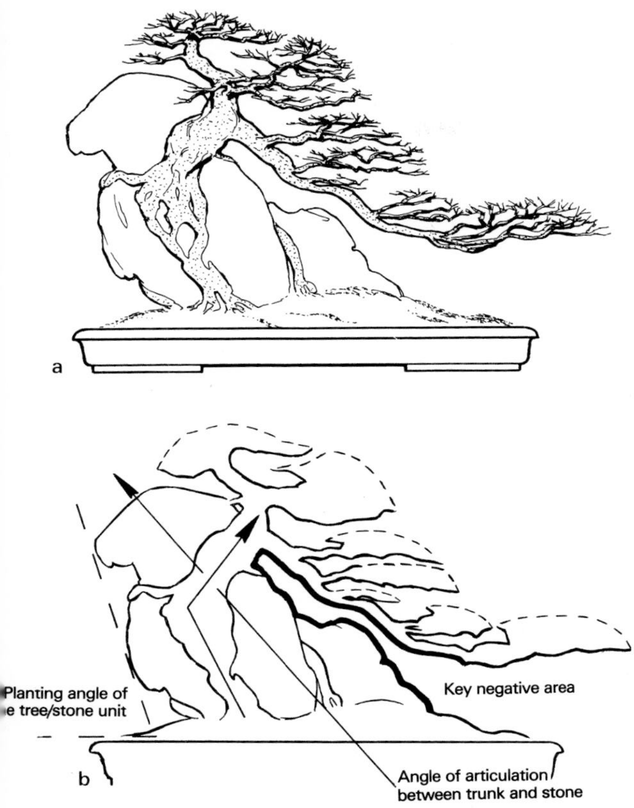

situation is different, however, so the principles are followed that best suit the arrangement; it is best not to adhere too closely to some favourite and remembered photograph.

Rocks for medium trees are usually horizontal, vertical (Fig. 15) or L-shaped. Height of stones varies, being chosen to blend with the design when complete, that is, when the design has evolved and matured. Make sure the height of the rock will remain in scale with the concept – it is easy to misjudge this.

Placement on horizontal stones is at one third the length or at the end but placement on vertical stones *can* be at the top *provided* the tree is well to one side with the bias sweeping down like a Cascade; however, more normal placement is at the two thirds point vertically, with the trunk base situated in from the edge.

Placement on L-shaped stones (Fig. 15b–d) is normally over the foot with the vertical behind the tree, often as a background, some-

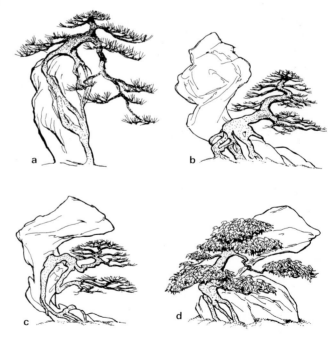

**Fig. 15** Style development: Root over stone. (a) Tree placement on vertical stone showing the less usual top position. (b) L-shaped stone with tree over the foot. (c) L-shaped stone with the form inverted. (d) Tree showing good complementary form that blends well with the stone.

**Fig. 14** Style development: Root over stone. (a) Usual medium-sized tree in the informal shape. (b) Same tree in diagrammatic form showing planting angle, angle of articulation and key negative area.

tree/stone unit. Both factors shape the negative area between the underside of the low branch and soil surface, which in this style is an important element of a pleasing design. The actual placement on the stone looks well if it occurs at one end or at a point one third along its length. The tree should not be dumped on to the top of the stone but should spring naturally from it.

Two other factors that help are the time spent assessing the stone, so that its best features are displayed and not covered up in planting, and determining the type of root pattern desired. This latter point is best established by referring to pictures and photographs of other similar Bonsai. Every

43

**Fig. 16** Style development: Root over stone. (*a*) 'Winter-viewing' tree. (*b*) Vertical stone 'old heavy trunk' variant. (*c*) 'Induction'. Note how the impact of the design differs through the use of different stones. (*d*) Tall tree multiple planting.

times distinct. The 'L' may be inverted in which case the tree may be planted at the side beneath the overhang as a repeat motif. Equally, the tree may be planted on the opposite side to the overhang.

As the planting matures it can be greatly refined if peripheries can be made to complement or conform to the shape of the stone. Domed, simple forms look well and if the planting features the low branch, this may be close to the canopy, extending it but removed by a vertical negative area, or, if remotely placed, the canopy form may be repeated in miniature. The trunk may be entire or divided into several leaders. Deciduous species such as Trident Maple are often grown for their distinctive winter display of branch masses. If a tree is to be grown for winter appreciation the trunk is often multi-leadered and carries a very full complement of branches and twigs.

These may be so closely placed as to look almost solid. The degree of twig density allowed or enjoyed is a personal thing but it will be seen that most winter display trees show several pronounced negative areas around trunk/branch junctions.

The initial ground/first branch negative area must be interestingly formed and downswept twigs (provided they make a substantial, not an irritatingly flimsy statement) may break into the area; root patterns at the side and base add shape and the ground pattern itself contributes something. With such a heavy canopy the provision of such visual relief space is important and it is a good thing if accompanying root patterns are simple.

Plantings on vertical stones (Fig. 16) have peripheries which are mainly domed but in this variant the form of the stone plays a far more assertive role. Often the rock may appear to function as an old heavy trunk with new branches. Where this illusion is created, rocks used are slender and the root formation heavy, to reinforce the feeling of the old trunk. This effect is obtained by placing the roots close together, within their separate bunches, so they eventually coalesce and knit together. The degree of root formation allowed should be carefully considered: with Trident Maples if a lot of separated root is featured, in time the stone almost vanishes due to the fantastic webbing of the roots. This effect if disliked, can be avoided by arranging root bunches closely together with distinct spacing between them. The spaced placement also preserves the exposed features of the stone and prevents their being masked by root spread.

It is best to arrange the canopies simply, to enhance the strength of the core. Branch deployment follows simplified Informal style rules. The placement of the tree affects the form: those trees planted at the top of the stone often show broad, flat root formation and a heavy foliage canopy with low branch; while those trees planted to one side often follow Cascade principles. The impression given also depends on the height of the stone; a solid mushroom can be made into an elegant Informal simply by adding height. The facility to effect change in a design by altering one factor is known as induction (Fig. 16c) and it is by this means that the subtlest alterations, modifications or refinements are achieved.

Plantings on L-shaped stones are made mainly to the side, when the 'L' is inverted, and are often smaller than the stone. The form is usually simple, foliage profiles are shallow domes, the head appearing alone or in association with the low branch. Root formations are essentially simple and usually appear as one or two broad, flat areas. The very simplicity of the style dictates exact placement and every element must be carefully considered. When the 'L' is the right way up, planting methods are as for the horizontal stone, but at the same time, the vertical must be exploited in the design. It may be thought of as a cliff with a shrub at the base, in which case the plant should be kept small and rounded or it may almost appear as a Jin through clouds of balled foliage. Very effective arrangements can be made using Junipers.

All the above combinations may be grown as winter viewing trees and as multiples with equal success.

TALL TREES

These look magnificent when grown as Upright single or multiple trunks (Fig. 16d). If there are a number of trunks, Group principles are reflected throughout. Placement of single trees is at one end or at one third along a flattish stone. Multiple trunk plantings are usually placed at one third but can be arranged over the stone so this remains as a central feature with the roots more or less clutching it equally. The effect of this latter variant is to minimize the scale of the stone which appears almost as a glorified pebble and the group itself as a clump arrangement. The classical tall planting tends to be narrow for its height thus enhancing the linear qualities of the trunk. The trunks are gently tapered and often slender and branches are arranged on triadic principles but there is a naturalness implicit in the variant that should be allowed to come through. Negative areas are of the usual importance and the initial vertical gap between root line and first branch is often a third of the total height. Secondary and tertiary negative areas remain generous enabling the eye to travel through and enjoy the structure. Apical areas are compact and interestingly formed. Branch peripheries echo this interest and foliage profiles may often be confined to the terminal third or half of the branch length. This arrangement opens the planting still further by emphasizing vertical negative areas and the quality of the trunk. Root patterns are simple and the broad flat root of Trident Maple is particularly appropriate and strengthens the natural, eroded-root feeling of this style. Foliage canopies look best when they are simply resolved and a broadly domed outline looks pleasant.

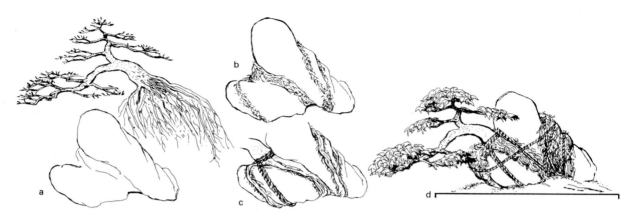

**Fig. 17** Style development: Root over stone: Method.
(*a*) Matching of tree and stone. (*b*) The stone prepared
with peat compost plastered over fissures. (*c*) The tree
seated temporarily tied. Roots arranged along compost
channels. (*d*) Arrangement complete.

## *Method*

Working in a cool, shaded area as bud activity
begins in the spring, tree and stone are first
matched together (Fig. 17). A rough idea can
be gained of the combined effect without
disturbing the tree and if the combination
looks promising the tree may be unpotted and
tried on the stone. Trees used have long roots
capable of completely embracing the stone,
and which have been produced by keeping the
tree in a deep container for a season.

When one is satisfied with the placement of
the tree, a sketch or an instant photograph to
assist the memory will be found useful.
Remove the tree, and keep the roots moist.
Prepare plenty of peat compost: one part
loam, two parts peat, mashed together with
water. Plaster the areas of the stone chosen for
the passage of the roots. Using a water jet,
remove all soil from the root mass, divide the
roots into bunches, and place the tree immediately the excess water has drained off.
Refer to the sketch or photograph, seat the
tree firmly and make sure the roots are divided
and placed according to the design. If the tree
is to be placed on the vertical wall of the stone
or any other awkward position, plenty of
temporary ties should be kept handy to support the base of the trunk. When one is happy
with the posture of the tree, check again to
ensure the base of the trunk is firmly in place
and tie this point securely with string or raffia.
Do *not* use nylon or wire, as the ties must rot
naturally. Do not use excessive pressure.

The roots are trained along the compost-
smeared crevices and secured with more compost. Use the fingers at all times. The tips of
the roots should pass under the stone. Add
moistened sphagnum or other moss – it
should be flat – and pat into good contact with
the mulch. Additional ties using string or
raffia are made where necessary to keep the
roots fully in contact with the stone, to soil
level. The tree and stone unit is then potted up
in the usual way and the root and moss area are
misted to maintain humidity. After the soil is
watered the tree is kept shaded for at least
three weeks. Plantings are tender till the roots
really establish so avoid extremes of weather.

CUTTINGS [EXAMPLE: MAPLE]
In the second year after establishment in a
deep container, the tree may be kept compact
by regular soft pruning. This is particularly
important where deciduous trees are concerned. Feed the tree well but watch for
overgrowths. If the tree is very vigorous and
simple soft pruning does not check the tree
sufficiently or produce enough secondary
shoots, the tips of the shoot and the first pair of

side leaves are trimmed away. This will check the tree and the additional foliage induced will cause the trunk to thicken.

Later in the season the cutting may be wire shaped (Fig. 18). The style followed is usually the Informal. The first bend is the major consideration as all subsequent bends are subsidiary. Do not forget to arrange the trunk three-dimensionally by raking the trunk line backwards and bending the top half forwards. Keep the upper portion of the tree pinched back hard and allow the lower branches to extend without pinching for the rest of the season. This extension of the lower area and apical foliage reduction, helps create taper. The lower branches are tipped back at the end of August but should remain three times the length of the apical area. Remove wires.

YEAR 3 In spring, the shaped cutting is transplanted into a large flat container with good depth, using a well-drained light compost. Heavy roots are removed or severely shortened and the system is evened to encourage the minor roots. The root system is spread as radially as possible.

In mid-season the tree is leaf cut and the stronger branches are arranged with wire (Fig. 18c). Apical branches after wiring are kept short and any overstrong shoots which appear with the new foliage are checked by using the shoot and side leaf removal technique (Fig. 18d). Feed the tree well throughout the season and trim and remove wires in August.

YEAR 4 In spring, the form of the tree is assessed. If it needs additional trunk and branch bulk it is transplanted and year 3 procedures are followed.

If the tree is deemed ready it may be transferred to the stone as described. If the

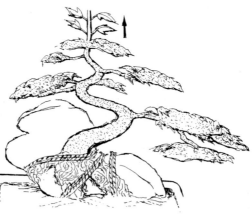

Fig. 18 Style development: Root over stone.
(a) Wire shaping. (b) The upper portion of the tree is reduced. (c) In year 3 the branches are arranged with wire. (d) Shoot and side-leaf removal technique. (e) The trunk may be thickened by allowing an apical shoot to extend.

trunk of this (or indeed any Bonsai) needs thickening, a shoot may be allowed to grow away at the apex (choose a rear one) and this rapidly extending shoot will help increase the diameter considerably. The shoot is removed in August. This system may be followed annually unless lower branches show weakness, in which case the shoot is removed immediately, and the upper regions of the tree pruned hard to restore the balance. Despite the drawbacks, the increase in diameter of the trunk makes the technique worthwhile. Use a deeper container than during year 3.

If trunk thickness is already acceptable, the tree may be grown as for year 3, and the terminal/side leaf removal technique is followed, working gradually over the tree. This technique should be phased over about a month and may be started in May. Inner portions of branches and those branches placed lower, are weaker than terminals and apical areas, therefore such weaker areas are normally allowed 2 to 3 pairs of leaves per shoot, whilst the stronger tips and higher areas are reduced to one pair of leaves. Any wiring necessary is carried out in mid-summer and removed in August with the annual trim back.

YEAR 5 The tree/stone unit is transplanted into the final container. The choice of design and shape is obviously dictated by the evolving tree, but generally, medium depth ovals or rectangles are best till the tree is complete. Root ties should have rotted long since, but it is worth checking to see if any remain. Be careful to support the stone underneath when repotting and preserve the long roots wrapped around it. Use an open, light soil.

The growing techniques are continued, but if the low branch is to be featured, the lower areas may be allowed to grow without pruning till mid-summer, when they are pruned back and wired. If this technique is followed for a few years, the low branch will thicken to the extent where it may almost become a second trunk.

YEAR 6 AND ONWARDS The tree is trans-planted every other year and the various trimming techniques are followed to build the desired peripheries. If the object is the winter display variant, the terminal/side leaf techniques are followed annually.

Cuttings intended for tall trees or groups over a stone are grown without wire shaping and they are assembled after two years. During the two-year development period they are kept compact by pinching. The leading shoot of each trunk is stopped about twice a year and a new leader selected from the resultant shoots; all others at the same point are removed. This checking helps trunk taper.

The tree or trees are planted over the stone in the spring of year 3. Style development follows that for Formal Upright – relaxed variant, or Group principles for the multiple trunk form. As the planting proceeds multiples are best supported with plenty of temporary ties. When the main trees are secured over the stone they may be temporarily tied to each other for extra support and the subsidiary trees supported in the same way. When all the tree bases have been secured over the stone with raffia, the temporary ties are released. Settling-in procedures are standard.

When watering, always remember that the large volume of stone present in the soil, plus the long pots used, create a lot of surface tension in the water content. All drainage aids are vital, cant the pot after watering if the soil remains unusually damp.

ROCKS AND STONES

These combine better if they are sober in colour. Pale colours declare themselves to the detriment of the unit. If tufa, for example, is weathered before use it is acceptable, but too often it appears in its raw cream state. There is good stone to be found in the UK and in suitable colours, textures, shapes and hardness. Dark greys, browns, dark reds and the slate family colours are best. Avoid metamorphic stone with a very smooth texture; the stone should evoke cliff texture and have definite creasing or a molecular nature. Strata follows the style of use: verticals should feature vertical fissures and so on. The stone must sit well, and if it does not, this may be rectified by chiselling the basal area or by joining on a buttress of sympathetically formed stone of the same type.

Do not use stones which are brittle, crumbly, or of the type that delaminate with frost.

## Root on Stone style (Ishizuki)

The trunk is variable in form and character as the variants of this style are so dissimilar. Variants include: small size, 7.5–10 cm (3–4 in); group variants; and the compact Informal type discussed in Root over Rock. The best material is available through cuttings and nursery stock.

The tree is planted in a hollow on a sympathetically shaped stone; they then become one unit and are never taken apart.

### *Applications*

Small Size Trees. Arranged on large landscape stones, these give an immediate impression of mountain scenery. Their very size in relation to the stone makes it seem enormous and this quality must be fully exploited. The tree shape best suited is the Formal and the trees are arranged according to the Group principles of perspective.

Horizontal stones properly used, give the effect of a plateau above the treeline, almost on top of a mountain (Fig. 19a). Stones with peaks and broad flattish areas are therefore appropriate – if not easy to find!

Ideally, placement of the plant material enhances and heightens the landscape qualities of the stone but does not obscure its best features. The planting may be seen quite simply as a foreground forest or as a single or series of clumps of diminishing size planted on contoured soil pockets, but all against a distant mountain. The clumps are separately stated and the overall periphery echoes the shape of the raised areas of the stone.

Another small tree arrangement that looks well is the Group displayed on a flat stone. Placement is very effective at the one-third point. Sometimes enormously long stones are

Fig. 19   Style development: Root on stone.
(*a*) Horizontal plateau stone. (*b*) The Atoll stone.
(*c*) Vertical stone.

used and the scale effect is quite extraordinary – the whole unit has the quality of a new atoll (Fig. 19b) with primary growth.

Vertical stone arrangements often seen are the inverted 'L' capped with forest (Fig. 19c), or flanked by a series of foliage steps that begin beneath the overhang and climb up, moving around the vertical to the top. These arrangements often feature triangular peripheries and relate to the stone and to each other.

GROUP VARIANTS
GROUPS ON FLAT STONES Many species and group variants are planted on the flat stone (Fig. 20a). Unquestionably the most popular stone shape for groups, the slab provides a very natural base and the linear form, a readily utilized coordinating element.

Placement of the plant material is usually with the main tree at one-third the stone's length. Arrangements follow usual Group principles and much enjoyment can be had making the plant material really blend with the stone. If the stone is very flat, formal arrangements with horizontal or rigidly

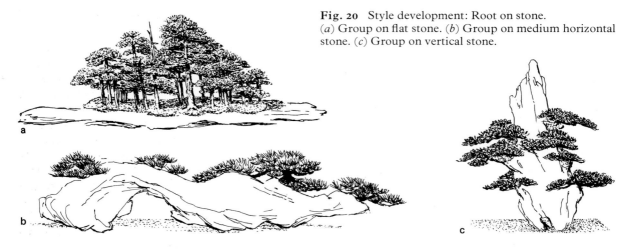

**Fig. 20** Style development: Root on stone. (*a*) Group on flat stone. (*b*) Group on medium horizontal stone. (*c*) Group on vertical stone.

downswept branches look handsome. More informal stones set off curving or windswept plantings to good effect.

GROUPS ON MEDIUM HORIZONTAL STONES (Fig. 20*b*) Long stones of medium height and a form reminiscent of capes and rock promontories are the most popular. Often the stone will feature an arch suggesting the erosion of the sea. If the group is planted with the bias to the end of the stone, remote from the bridge, and the peripheries are kept low, hugging the stone, the effect is immediately one of sea and cliff. Variations on this theme are popular in Japan at the moment and there are several famous plantings of hedgehog Pines or Junipers on dramatic cape stones.

GROUPS ON VERTICAL STONES These stones (Fig. 20*c*), based on natural formations such as the limestone hills of Guilin in China, dominate the plant material. Once again, scale is important and fine-textured plants such as Cotoneaster, dwarf Azalea or Spruce are appropriate. The principle follows the old trunk variant and outcropping on the stone should be subtly reinforced with low, rounded plant forms. Groups in the loosest sense, the foliage areas follow common foliage profiles and usually consist of one main species with a subsidiary accent planting. The plant clumps echo and relate to each other but the detail is played down so the stone always appears simple and unfussy.

INFORMAL Apart from the greater emphasis on the shape of the stone, the comments on style given for Informal Root over Stone are applicable. The low branch variant may be grown on a very long stone in which case the branch echoes the length with very dramatic effect.

The development of plant material follows that for Root over Stone with one major difference: long roots are always discouraged and the root mass kept compact, shallow training containers being used for the same reason.

NURSERY STOCK AND CUTTINGS
Young nursery stock can be used successfully but older material does not adapt so easily to the radical reduction of soil and root, neither does an aged root system attach to and adopt the rock so well. If very desirable older material is found, it is best to transplant it annually for three or four seasons using shallow containers to encourage a younger type of root system.

The tree may legitimately be very squat and spreading in this style. Low, rounded profiles are suited to all the stone shapes but look superb with vertical and bridge stones.

Cuttings are easily trained to this shape by successively removing vertical shoots and encouraging laterals. Lower branches are allowed great length before trimming back in August and this makes powerful, heavy-trunked trees with stout lower branches. All hanging foliage is removed from branch lines and this simple technique gives the 'buns' a more tree-like appearance as the structures are revealed.

## Method

Proceed as for the Root over stone style and record the exact position of the tree. Remove tree; the roots must be anchored on the planting zone till they have developed and so the unit must be wired. Begin by making wire loops and secure these to the periphery of the planting zone. The loops may be secured to the stone by the use of lead strip which is wrapped round each loop base (Fig. 21a) and then punched into a crevice. Should no crevices be available, holes may be drilled. Epoxy glue or fibreglass are other means by which the loops can be secured.

Plastic-covered wires, long enough to meet over the chosen point, are tied to the loops and draped out of the way (Fig. 21b). Peat compost is prepared using equal parts of loam and peat mixed with water. Plaster the chosen area generously. Wash the whole root mass if it refuses to sit properly, otherwise retain a little soil around the trunk. Spread the root mass as evenly as possible and tie the tree by twisting the first pair of wires over the root near the trunk (Fig. 21c). This will support the tree while the roots are worked gently into the compost with the fingers. Twist-tie all remaining wires. If the weight, position or leverage call for firm tying, ensure that major friction points are cushioned with a piece of cycle inner tube or something similar. The firmness mentioned is relative – remember the roots are living entities – the wires should

**Fig. 21** Style development: Root on stone: Method.
(a) Lead strip wrapped around loop base prior to punching in. (b) Strings in place; planting zones plastered with peat cmpost. (c) Note the harmony between the trees and how they repeat each other – almost. (d) The completed arrangement. In left-hand tree, the tie wires are being secured; the right-hand tree has been secured and final moss cladding is in place.

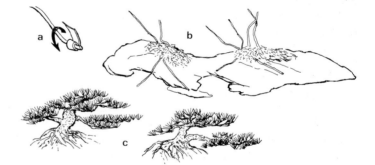

make no more than even contact. If the root mass swings down and undershoots any major projection, or is sited where gravitational pull threatens to dislodge it, the mass may be stabilized by encasing it in fine net tied to the original wire loops. Nylon or terylene net is ideal. Additional peat compost is added to the root system and if net is used, the compost goes on first.

Fine moss well soaked in water is now pressed into the compost. This is begun around the trunk, depressing compost and moss in the gaps between each of the main surface roots. The roots then appear to rise and grip the stone. Further moss is added until the mass is covered. Check that no artificial aids still show. Try to make the mossed area harmoniously contoured with the stone.

The whole unit is syringed with water, beginning with the mossed compost area and is placed in shade away from direct weather. Root on stone plantings need high humidity and even after the initial settlement period, watering is carefully maintained. The Japanese grow such plantings over humidifying areas of water, the stone being kept from direct water contact by concealed blocks, or it may be bedded in gravel which is kept damp.

Once formed, tree and stone are not usually taken apart. Repotting as such does not happen because roots usually penetrate the stone making it impossible; instead the root mass is blasted with water and new soil is pushed in around the system. However, if very hard or smooth stones are used, the chances of roots binding to them are reduced and a normal repot will be possible in such a case. One would simply untie the wires and repeat the initial process. The season for either method is spring.

## Twin Trunk style (Sokan)
The most important aspect of this style, as far as the trunk is concerned is the difference in diameter between the two. Suitable material is available through natural material and cuttings.

NATURAL MATERIAL
Examples of practically any species may be found in the UK. Birch, Beech (Fig. 22a–b), Hornbeam and Pine in particular provide good material.

**Fig. 22** Style development: Twin trunk.
(a) Natural tree, Beech, just after collection. (b) Same tree after styling and 2–3 years' growth. The growth alternates between the trunks and the two preserve their identity through the central negative area.
(c) Twin trunk reverse repeat motif.

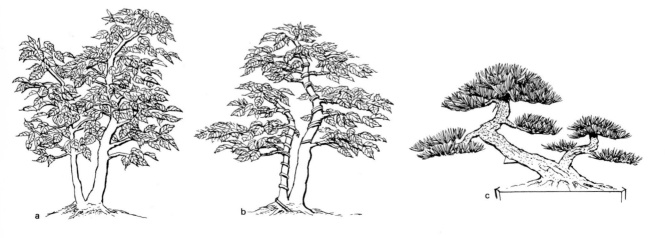

The style affords an opportunity for a really studied exercise in parallel disposition and placement. The trunks must be of sympathetic form and this is established by wiring where necessary; diameter increase of the main trunk if too similar to the minor; clearly defined negative areas and a sense of perspective between the two trunks. Branch lines are planned at this time and extraneous material is removed. Extraneous material is any that does not strengthen the basic, triadic placement. Exceptions are those branches retained simply to increase trunk diameter.

Diameter increase is controlled partly by regulating foliage density: the heavier the mass, the greater the diameter. The initial branch thinning must duly reinforce this factor. After the branch disposition is planned, the tree is transferred to the ground or a large temporary container and is well fed, a strongly growing vertical shoot being left to fatten the trunk quickly. If the dominance of the vertical shoot seriously retards lower branch development it is removed at once. The vertical shoot is never considered part of the design and is grown from the back so the removal scar is hidden. The shoot may be allowed to develop each year if all seems well through the structure, and heavily-trunked trees are soon produced.

If such a method is unpalatable, the regulation of foliage weight will achieve the same result over a longer period. Major trunks are permitted a hirsute appearance for a couple of seasons and minor trunks are kept meagrely clad. Every third year, or less if distress is seen anywhere, the heavier trunks are firmly discouraged and the minor trunks fattened up with free growth. It might be well to adopt an alternate yearly system.

TRUNK FORM The Twin Trunk is a form where the elements are in repose but where the detail may follow the shapes of another style. The average Twin Trunk is classifiable as Informal, but could equally well be trained as Slanting, Windswept, Literati, Driftwood and so on.

The essence of the Twin Trunk is mutual harmony. The major trunk may exceed by two or three times the height and complexity of the minor, but it is the feeling of integration between the two that satisfies. Trunk lines resemble and closely align with each other but preserve their own identities. Inner trunk lines should be simply seen for about two thirds of the height, and outer lines bear the structure – it is a simple exercise in group styling.

The horizontal negative area must not be too wide as this defeats the rhythm. By the nature of the arrangement the canopy of the bigger trunk will overhang the smaller, so to avoid problems of visual conflict and overshading, it is usual to preserve a broad, vertical negative area between the crown of the minor and the first adjacent branch of the main trunk. The branch in question is usually kept short to minimize conflict.

BRANCH DISPOSITION Branches may follow triadic placement but can alternate from major to minor trunk and back again, thus creating a fascinating combination of lines and mass. There are many classical Trident Maples trained after this principle. The other main system is where the minor trunk repeats the theme of the major, but in reverse (Fig. 22c). The feeling of integration is guaranteed and perspective is greatly enhanced where remoteness between the two is preserved. Examples of this may be seen among Pines, Junipers and Zelkovas.

CUTTINGS AND LAYERINGS
After establishment, if cuttings are beheaded just above ground level, the resultant mass of shoots is easily encouraged to yield two well-placed limbs. All other shoots are removed in the Twin style (Fig. 23a–b). The same technique may be used for raising connected multiples and here obviously, more shoots are retained.

Development for the next season follows the techniques used to increase the trunk diameter. Wiring may be carried out in the first season if growth is strong enough, using covered wires (Fig. 23d). Both trunks are

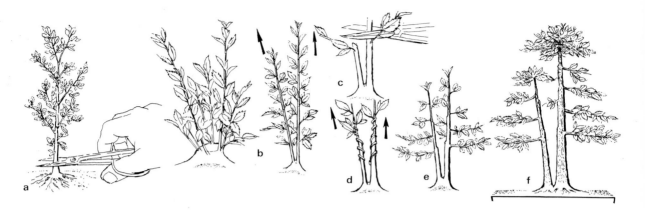

**Fig. 23** Style development: Twin trunk.
Twin trunk from cuttings – Chinese Elm. (*a*) Cutting is beheaded at ground level. (*b*) Resultant growths are reduced to two and grown on. (*c*) Growths are pruned. (*d*) Replacement spurs are wired into place and grown on. (*e*) The tree shows taper by the end of year 2. (*f*) The tree after 6–7 years' growth.

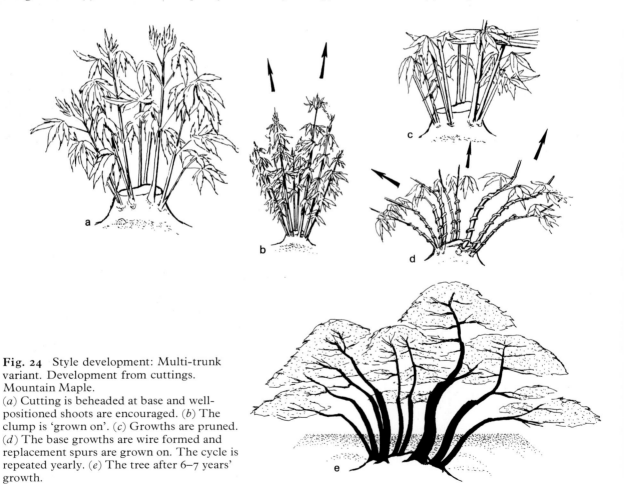

**Fig. 24** Style development: Multi-trunk variant. Development from cuttings. Mountain Maple.
(*a*) Cutting is beheaded at base and well-positioned shoots are encouraged. (*b*) The clump is 'grown on'. (*c*) Growths are pruned. (*d*) The base growths are wire formed and replacement spurs are grown on. The cycle is repeated yearly. (*e*) The tree after 6–7 years' growth.

54

trimmed back in August. During year 2 and subsequent years (Fig. 23*e–f*), the plant is well fed and judiciously trimmed, using feed and trimming like accelerator and brakes to balance and adjust diameter. With a fast growing subject such as Trident Maple or Chinese Elm the techniques followed will yield heavy trunks quickly, but taper will only be achieved if the tree is repeatedly shortened. A yearly maximum of something like 7.5 cm (3 in) periphery extension will give nice taper and avoid too many major 'chops'.

## Triple, Five, Seven Trunk Variants and Clumps

If one follows the principles of the Twin Trunk in combination with those for the Group, all these styles are easily raised and are really multi-trunked variants (Fig. 24*a–e*) of the Twin. The extra trunks give one the opportunity to design plantings with greater depth. The differences in trunk diameter become more important as the varying thicknesses create their own interest. Figure 25 shows three- and five-trunk styles. A diagonal axial line is very effective in creating the illusion of space.

**Fig. 25**  Style development: Multi-trunk variant.
(*a*) Three trunk style, Yew. (*b*) Five trunk style, Beech.

## Raft style (Ikadabuki)

The trunk may be slender and with many curves, or short and thick, the choice depending on the nature of the desired effect. The function of the trunk is to provide a firm, running buttress. Good material is available through natural material and nursery stock.

### *Applications*

The Raft is very much a style where the narrow trunk base controls other elements. If the trunk base is compact and powerful, its branches/trees are firmly set in a simple row. This may be called the straight line variant.

STRAIGHT LINE VARIANT

Pines, Junipers, Cryptomeria and Spruce look superb in this arrangement. The main tree sets the style and the flanking trees explore the theme in varied ways. The overall periphery is simple, consisting of a broad dome or pyramid (Fig. 26*a–c*), or perhaps a major canopy and an answering repeat. The trunks are usually upright or slanting. If there is movement all the trunks show and echo it. Initial trunk to first branch negative areas are clearly defined to emphasize the basal trunk

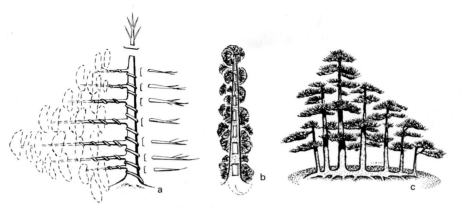

Fig. 26 Style development: Raft: Straight line variant. (*a*) Year before planting. Branches on downward face are removed and others shaped with wire. (*b*) Year of planting. View from below showing bark flaps removed prior to planting. (*c*) The planting after 10–15 years.

and individual 'tree trunk' quality. Horizontal negative areas between trees are emphatic enough to separate and suggest the grouping of forms. Arrangements of three to five trunks are effective. The actual shaping of the trees reflects the influence of other styles.

CURVED LINE VARIANT

The trunk base is normally snake-like and the branches/trees follow the linear form but the planting has greater depth due to the twists of the base (Fig. 27*a*–*c*). Tree forms are curving and usually informal.

*Method*

It is best to treat the tree a year before planting. The face of the trunk most favoured with branches will be uppermost. Branches growing on the remote side are best pruned as

these prevent the trunk from laying down properly. Branches at the sides may be wired out from the sides with their tips elevated. Straight line trunks are better without these side branches – simply wire shape the central spine limbs to the projected design. The trunk is wire shaped if necessary. During the pre-planting season all apical branches are kept small to encourage diameter increase in the low branches.

Year 2 begins with the preparation of a large container big enough to accept the whole unit. All wires are removed. Using a scalpel, oblong

Fig. 27 Style development: Raft: Curved line variant. (*a*) Year before planting. Branches on downward face are removed and others shaped with wire. (*b*) Year of planting. View from below showing bark flaps removed prior to planting. (*c*) The planting after 10–15 years.

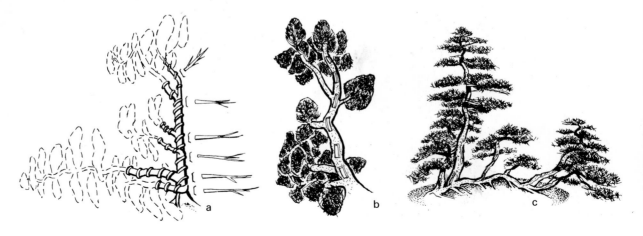

**Colour Plate 27.** Below: Slanting style
Scots Pine. 40–50 years.
**Colour Plate 28.** Left: Winter 1987/88.
60 years.

**Colour Plate 29.** Above: Driftwood style
Chinese Juniper. 100 years.
**Colour Plate 30.** Left: Winter 1986/87.
110 years.

**Colour Plate 31.** Below: Tree on Stone style Sloe. 25 years.
**Colour Plate 32.** Left: Twin Trunk style Scots Pine Yatsubusa 'Watereri'.
**Colour Plate 33.** Opposite: Winter 1986/87.
**Colour Plate 34.** Bottom: Cascade style Common Juniper. 80 years. From natural material.

**Colour Plate 35.** Above: Twin Trunk style Needle Juniper. 90 years.
**Colour Plate 36.** Left: Winter 1986/87. 100 years.

**Plate 17** (*above*)  Raft style Trident Maple.
Approximately 90 years old, imported tree. Height
48 cm (1 ft 7 in), spread 96 cm (3 ft 2⅜ in) trunk base
9 cm (3½ in). Unglazed pale brown oval.

**Plate 18** (*below*)  Root connected style Kyohime
Maple, Yatsubusa cv. of the Mountain Maple.
Approximately 25 years imported tree. Height 36 cm
(1 ft 2⅜ in) spread 72 cm (2 ft 4¾ in). Glazed off-white oval.

**Plate 19** Twin trunk style Japanese Hornbeam. Approximately 50 years. Height 79 cm (2 ft 7½ in) spread 83 cm (2 ft 8¼ in). Temporary training pot.

**Plate 20** Rear view. Close-up showing old rotted central trunk.

**Plate 21** Driftwood style Chinese Juniper. Unglazed
grey rectangle. Discussed in Evolution in Design.

flaps of bark are cut and removed on the underside of the trunk. The bark flaps are taken near old branch bases. The peeled areas must not exceed one third of the diameter in width and may be 2.5 cm (1 in) in length. The exposed sap wood is immediately dusted with hormone rooting powder. The tree is laid flat on a bed of specially prepared light soil in the container. If perspective is planned the main axis may be diagonal. Cover the recumbent trunk to a depth of 1.25 cm ($\frac{1}{2}$ in) or so and heap soil over the root mass. The root mass may be teased out prior to the planting to seat it down. Adjust the arrangement so that any tilting and angling are satisfactory. Check that branch/tree terminals are emerging correctly. Water in well. Protect in the usual way and do not shift the container once placed.

A month after planting the Raft may be fed. Pruning is not usually necessary during the first year but should apical areas of the recumbent trunk grow strongly they must be pruned hard to maintain a balance.

If young material is used it is possible for rooting to occur all along the trunk in one season, but normally it is safer to allow two seasons growth and to inspect the roots in the Spring of the third year. The plant is removed from the container and the soil is washed. New roots should equal the basal mass and if they do not, the basal mass is heavily pruned and the planting is given another season in the box.

If the new roots are satisfactory, the old root mass is cut off and the Raft may be transplanted to a suitable Bonsai pot. The pot should be deep enough to provide plenty of moisture. If only very shallow pots are available do not risk it – put the Raft back in the large container for another season to strengthen the root system. Using the techniques discussed under Soft Pruning, branch/trees are built up slowly.

## Root Connected style (Netsuranari)

The trunks in this style are in fact sprouts from running roots. Inspired by suckering species, the style is easily raised and sits more naturally than the Raft. The best material comes from layerings and natural material. Applications are very similar to those of the Raft and the Group. This is a good style for trees with dainty characteristics such as the dwarf Maples.

*Method*

An easily rooted subject such as Cypress or Maple is tip-layered beneath a branch whorl. When the layering has taken it is established in a deep, broad container using light soil. The central or original leader may be pruned away to encourage the lateral branches. After one month the planting is fed. During the first season no training is attempted beyond tidying peripheries of individual branches.

YEAR 2 In March the layering is removed from the container and covered wires are coiled loosely round the bases and up the branches. Using predetermined placing, the branch bases are arranged in a radial fashion around the centre and their terminals are elevated (Fig. 28b–c). The effect is immediately that of a three dimensional coppice. The layering is replaced in fresh soil in the container. Light root trimming may be necessary to even the system. After one month the planting is fed and shoot pinching is carried out for density and taper. Leading shoots on lateral branches are not pinched out if a tall group is envisaged, thus allowing the terminals stronger growth.

The wires should be examined weekly for any signs of causing constriction and should be cut immediately if this occurs – otherwise they are removed with the annual trimback in August. During mid-summer all emerging trees may be foliage thinned to emphasize and establish the desired form (Fig. 28d–e). Diameter increase is monitored in the usual way.

YEAR 3 In March the evolving Root Connected group may be transplanted into a more suitable container using the same light soil. Feeding is as before. During mid-summer the new side branches are arranged with wire and foliage is again thinned (Fig. 28f). Attention is paid to the foliage profiles.

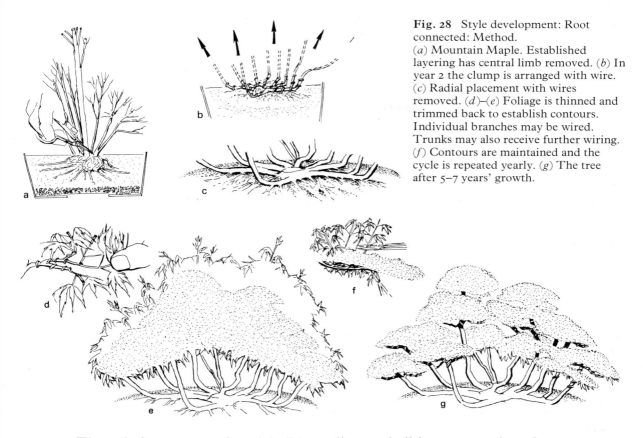

**Fig. 28** Style development: Root connected: Method.
(*a*) Mountain Maple. Established layering has central limb removed. (*b*) In year 2 the clump is arranged with wire. (*c*) Radial placement with wires removed. (*d*)–(*e*) Foliage is thinned and trimmed back to establish contours. Individual branches may be wired. Trunks may also receive further wiring. (*f*) Contours are maintained and the cycle is repeated yearly. (*g*) The tree after 5–7 years' growth.

YEAR 4 The techniques are continued, building the tree slowly and in about five to seven years from layering a very acceptable group will be formed (Fig. 28*g*).

NATURAL MATERIAL
It is worth foraging in hedgerows for natural material as this can be very promising. Once secured, prepare a large container, establish the planting and arrange with wire in the following year. After this follow the standard techniques.

## Group style (Yose Ue)
Trunk forms show variation on the theme of the major tree and most Groups feature at least one other large tree which is secondary only to the major. Choosing these two therefore really determines the nature of the Group, all other trunks being subsidiary.

### *Applications*
The previous single unit, multi-stem styles discussed all have one major advantage over the Yose Ue (assembled tree group), and that is total uniformity of foliage and growth rate. When assembling the separate trees therefore it is of enormous help if they are known to be propagated by cuttings or layerings of identical material source. Seedlings are not to be trusted; their variability is notorious. Cloning of material is vital if superior Bonsai are to be made. The Zelkova Broom group has been fully discussed and a few other popular Group variants are included.

LOW SPRUCE GROUP
This variant is single, or doubly triangular (Fig. 29*a*) in periphery and included in the mass are two or three interrelated, subsidiary triangles. The horizontal measurement is approximately twice or more that of the height and a planting 105–120 cm (3½–4 ft) long, often features a primary apex of 45 cm (1½ ft) and a secondary apex of 30 cm (1 ft). Assuming such a planting comprises around 35

**Fig. 29** Style development: Group.
Low Spruce Group. Note how the visual speed of the trunks is stabilized by the triangular
periphery or rhythm. The texture is equal through foliage and ground cover and is terminated by the quiet base
which slows everything down.

trunks, approximately 21 or so will be in the primary group and the remainder in the secondary.

Lines of the trunks, and the tensions and visual speed created (Fig. 29*b*), the negative areas related both vertically and horizontally, all follow the principles already discussed for the Zelkova Broom group. In other words, placement and spatial relationships remain similar and emphasis is achieved by dominant diameter/height accents, or by closer or wider negative areas.

In the Spruce, Cypress, Cryptomeria and Pine groups, foliage lines are horizontal and downswept, and domed, triangular or flat in section. Rear low and slender trunks placed for perspective create far better depth in evergreen groups because of the refinement of the permanent shape, therefore work of great subtlety can be achieved with these species.

CYPRESS AND CRYPTOMERIA GROUPS
These both give the opportunity for groups that follow the Zelkova Broom group layout but the form is truly triangular (Fig. 30) and may appear as two or more interrelative forms, or even as one. Trees follow Formal Upright principles with acknowledgment to their Group function, which is that major forward and central trees are free of lower

**Fig. 30** Style development: Group.
Cryptomeria Group. Note how the visual speed is greatest through the horizontal movement of branches and this time is stabilized by the simple trunk structure. The periphery slows the rhythm by providing further stable triangles within the overall triangular form.

The texture of the foliage is absorbed by the quiet earth pattern and terminated by the simple pot line.

foliage; outer trees, at both left and right, have inner facing foliage removed, and that lower trees are placed usually to the rear where the foliage can be appreciated as a foil to the trunks.

## PINE GROUPS

These are the object of such widely differing treatment both as Yose Ue, Raft and Root Connected, that practically every style and variant is represented except Broom. The actual placement follows standard principles.

One of the first considerations affecting the style of group is the sensation of scale afforded by the needle length of the chosen clone of Pine. The Japanese currently tend to favour small-leaved cultivars of Pine which are specially bred for Bonsai and go under the general description of Yatsubusa. This *roughly* means a neat growing plant that takes kindly to pruning and one which will produce adventitious buds as a result. There are cultivars of the Scots Pine that can well be designated Yatsubusa for Bonsai purposes: *Pinus sylvestris* var. *beuvronensis* (Fig. 31a) and *P. s.* var. *wateriana* are good examples. Both are popular subjects for rockeries but are little known as Bonsai. Such small-leaved Pines obviously increase flexibility in the design of the Group as tiny foliage enhances perspect-

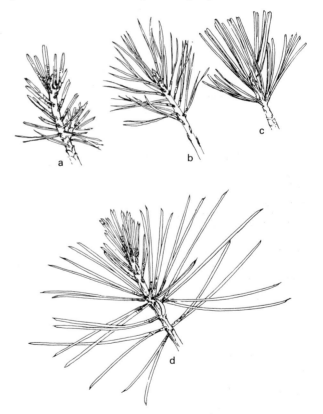

**Fig. 31** Style development: Group.
Pine Groups: relative needle sizes. (*a*) Yatsubusa form, *Pinus sylvestris* 'Beuvronensis'. (*b*) *Pinus sylvestris*. (*c*) *Pinus parviflora*. (*d*) *Pinus thunbergii*.

ive. Both species will produce leaves of 2.5 cm (1 in) or under.

The next most desirable species in terms of scale are the Japanese Five-Needle and the Scots Pine type: *Pinus parviflora* (Fig. 31c) and *P. sylvestris*. Both species have leaves of 5–8 cm (2–3 in) in nature, which reduce to a little over 2.5 cm (1 in) with good Bonsai culture. Varieties with slightly curved or twisted needles can be used because with time the shoot pruning practised in Bonsai will straighten the leaves. Straight-leaved forms are always superior.

The last of the popular Pine types is the Japanese Black: *Pinus thunbergii*. This is the trickiest to handle in a Group, as in nature the leaves are 7–10 cm (3–4 in) in length and despite careful pruning, it is difficult to ensure even needle development. Needles on imported Black Pines are frequently cut in half, so it seems to be a world-wide problem! It is possible to reduce needle size to 2.5 cm (1 in) but uniformity of length is difficult to accomplish and maintain in a group of individual trees. Once again, the Cluster variants score.

Yatsubusa Pines are ideally suited to low-growing plantings (Fig. 32a) with a height of between 30 cm (1 ft) and 45 cm (1½ ft). They also look well when smaller, up to 15 cm (6 in), in pots or on rocks. The Japanese Yatsubusa cultivars (Fig. 32b) usually appear as Clump style variants rather than as Yose Ue.

The Japanese Five-Needle and Scots Pine

(Fig. 33) give a good overall effect at between 30 cm (1 ft) and 60 cm (2 ft) as this is big enough for bark, fine twigs and roots to be fully appreciated in relative proportion.

The Black Pine must be around 60 cm (2 ft) to be really successful otherwise the needle length defeats perspective and confuses the branch line, or even worse, in an effort to

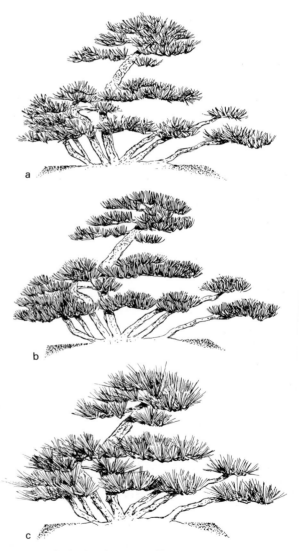

Fig. 33 Style development: Group. Pine Groups: impact made by scale. The same group demonstrating the differences in design caused by needle texture. The imaginary group is 60 cm (2 ft 8 in) in height in: (*a*) *Pinus sylvestris*. (*b*) *Pinus parviflora*. (*c*) *Pinus thunbergii*.

Fig. 32 Style development: Group. Pine Groups: impact made by scale. (*a*) *Pinus sylvestris* 'Beuvronensis', height 45 cm (18 in). (*b*) Japanese Yatsubusa form, height 20 cm (8 in).

correct this, the whole plant is subject to artificial topiary and looks as natural as a clipped poodle.

## BEECH AND HORNBEAM GROUPS

The Japanese White Beech Group is assembled really to appreciate trunks and bark quality, as is the Hornbeam. Resolved twig detail is usually lacking with the Beech and better, but not vastly improved, with the Hornbeam. It is the *impression* given by Groups of both species and the winter form (Fig. 34) which is important. In leaf it is difficult to avoid an unbroken mass which becomes heavy when looked at for any length of time. Placement principles are standard and there is more than usual emphasis on diameter and height differences. Peripheries are usually simple triangles or domes.

## TRIDENT AND MOUNTAIN MAPLE GROUPS

Both species have such good bark, roots, twigs and leaves, that in or out of leaf and at any size, they possess *all* the attributes of a good group. As with the Pine, they are the object of every conceivable variant in style, whilst following standard placement principles.

The Trident is seen more often than the Mountain as an assembled group, because of its greater strength. With separate trees, the survival of the weakest in competition with the fittest and biggest is always a problem. The Mountain Maple appears most frequently in group form as a Clump, Raft or Root Connected variant, as these are easier to manage.

Currently, the Trident is being grown a great deal as a group of 15 or more trees with a height of 65 cm (2 ft 2 in) or so, featuring two or three dominant trunks. Such arrangements are, in the main, straight-trunked and with good taper. Overall peripheries are frequently deeply domed and the foliage carried high, leaving 50% of the lower trunks exposed.

Placement is akin to the Zelkova Broom group. The Trident Maple possesses enormous vigour and a strongly vertical growth habit and this may be carefully exploited to

**Fig. 34** Style development: Group. Japanese Hornbeam Group in winter.

give interesting kinks in the trunk by pruning and allowing the chosen replacement bud unlimited extension. The pruned trunk soon swells out to compensate for the diameter difference but the kink is not swallowed but remains as a natural change of movement. Quite a different effect is gained if pruning is delayed till August and the trunk is trimmed back to an outer facing bud. New growth in the Spring replaces the caliper much more slowly and the 'chop' remains as a sharp change of movement. In the straight-trunked Trident Maple Group, up to half of the trunks will have been treated in these ways at least once.

The hard trunk pruning technique contributes another aspect unique to these groups, namely the termination of outer trunks to create inverted 'L' forms. The entire outline ascends in a series of outer pointing steps occasioned by the various enforced changes of line. Negative areas are preserved by training the emerging side branches and twigs to conform to the new line. The new head of each outer trunk is wedge sectioned. The primary change of plane junction is usually free of twigs, a simple, angular form which ramifies in three increments to a broad, and densely-twigged peripheral segment. Heads of centrally placed and major trees are domed, with ninety percent of their branches confined to the upper trunk.

The dense twig habit of Trident Maple

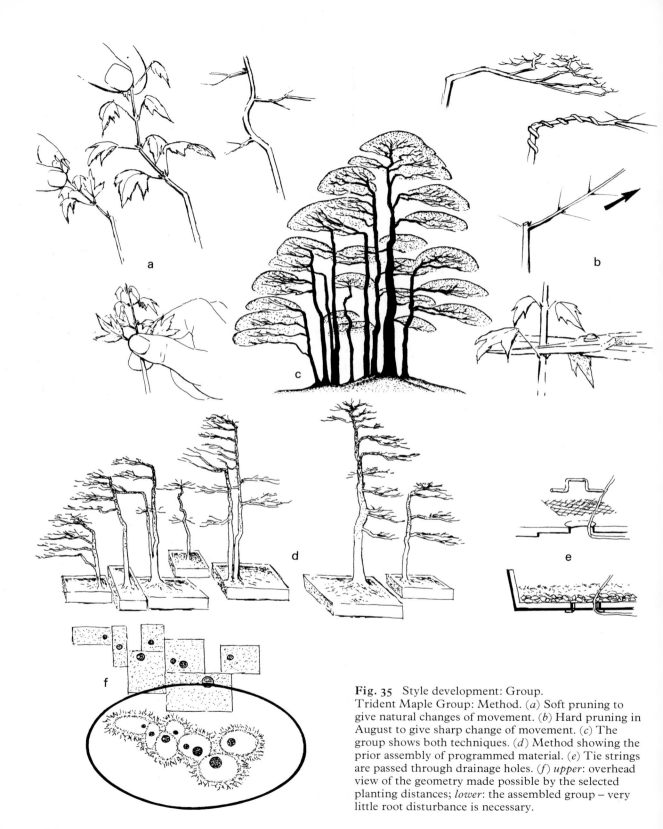

**Fig. 35** Style development: Group.
Trident Maple Group: Method. (*a*) Soft pruning to give natural changes of movement. (*b*) Hard pruning in August to give sharp change of movement. (*c*) The group shows both techniques. (*d*) Method showing the prior assembly of programmed material. (*e*) Tie strings are passed through drainage holes. (*f*) *upper*: overhead view of the geometry made possible by the selected planting distances; *lower*: the assembled group – very little root disturbance is necessary.

makes the winter shape of major interest. It is also possible by regulation of the same twig and foliage weight, to emphasize trunk diameter and peripheral density and balance them against negative areas so quickly, in terms of Bonsai development, that the design really approaches painting in the possibilities, refinements and juggling of the components. Thus, when successful, it is the winter shape that satisfies, where every element is in balance, rather than the leafed form.

The Mountain Maple group is a curving and graceful Bonsai; it has refinement both in form and colour balance between silver-buff old bark, and the fresh green and red of the twigs. The style followed is Informal Upright with the difference that heads and branches are spread in an upcurving manner, the effect being that of a champagne glass. Placement is standard. It bears repeating that Clump variants are more easily maintained.

*Method*
It is always desirable to pretrain material destined for Group work. When using cuttings or seedlings they may be assembled after their first transplanting as basic nuclear clumps. It is still desirable to follow the techniques suggested for relative trunk fattening (under Zelkova Broom groups) for two or three seasons (Fig. 35), so the clump should not consist of more than three trunks. This also avoids precise duplication of trunk diameter. It is helpful if containers of the same *depth* are used, regardless of other dimensions, so a very approximate idea might be gained of plan and side elevation placement by moving containers around at eye level (Fig. 35*d*). This also serves to give an idea of how branch tiers, heights, shapes and peripheries are developing.

Early clump assembly permits close placement of trunks within the unit, which is very desirable and much more difficult to achieve with established root masses. It also helps if clumps which are destined to be closely adjacent are planted towards one edge of the temporary container – the one-sided root permits butting. Where negative areas are critical, such as a horizontal division between primary and secondary nuclei, this may be precisely determined. Simply divide the desired gap by two and ensure the relevant clumps are each planted at half this measured distance from the edge of their containers. Check to see the future butted edge of the clump is adjacent to the temporary container edge.

The assembly of such programmed material (Fig. 36) is a joy and carries the bonus of an instant, natural appearance with plant health assured and a large proportion of the finer points of group work already accomplished.

Groups are assembled as Spring begins. Each tree is root pruned according to size and vigour. Remember that little trees need all the help they can get and be gentle. Major trees are pruned harder but never take more than a sixth of the total mass. Do not part the clumps. Set each tree and clump aside according to position and cover the roots with wet sphagnum moss.

Prepare a large temporary container big

**Fig. 36** Style development: Group. Trident Maple Group: Method. Major trees are placed first and subsidiary ones follow when the 'key' features work together.

enough to accept and complement the entire group. Groups always need complementary space, amounting to half to two-thirds of the ground pattern occupied by the trunks. It also makes good sense with regard to plant health to give the extra root run at this time. Soil depth is critical: the average Maple Group for example needs at least two inches of depth to remain turgid. This may be added to at final potting by soil mounding.

The transplanting and growth cycle will ensure flat root systems but tying-in strings are a boon. Check the drainage holes and introduce more if necessary. Long containers mean a lot of surface tension in the water, so every device to aid drainage should be used. The container may be of wood or a plastic seed tray may be used, secure crocking discs over the drainage holes, then secure polythene strings or covered wire up through the holes to facilitate tying in. Bare wire kills roots.

A mesh grid made of split-bamboo greenhouse stakes, tied at each cross-member, may be found useful to locate trees if they are very tall and heavily trunked. This sits on the drainage course and is secured through the drainage holes. The drainage course comprises large-particled, sieved grit and should be of generous depth. A bottom layer of soil is added – well sieved, dry, and of coarse texture.

The major trees are planted first. If any eminence is planned to emphasize group structure and perspective, it is added now: simply add soil and try the trees on it till the desired differentials are reached. Remember, the main tree is located one-third along the length of the main axis and forward of centre along the minor axis. Check placement, angle, elevation and adjust. Make sure – without pounding the root or impacting the soil – that the trees sit well and are stable. Fingers are better than sticks. Tie the clumps. Assemble secondary and tertiary points, and when you are satisfied that they all articulate correctly, work slowly round each focal point adding subsidiary trees in accordance with the design, and tying as the work progresses. Always check in minutest detail that everything co-ordinates. When the relative heights and negative areas are established, the final contouring of the soil is completed. As coarse soil has been used throughout, a finely textured top dressing can be added or a fine moss planted around major roots. This is purely for prettiness – do not cover all the soil – it is vital to see how it is behaving. Water in well, soil first, otherwise the drag weight topples the planting. Aftercare is standard. The group is transferred to the final container after two seasons. The group is always treated as a unit at repotting time.

If and where the grid is used, additional strings support each clump from at least four points, but if the grid is still insufficient, the pot may be encased in a supporting cage of vertical wires. Thick aluminium or copper wires are passed under the major and minor axis of the pot and right-angled upward with pliers. Thick wires are run horizontally between the uprights and looped and the cage becomes rigid. The offending trunks are stabilized by cross-tying to opposing uprights. Use covered wires and soften trunk friction points.

# 2 Material for Bonsai

## Cuttings

The snag is in finding the stock plant. A lot of plants in Bonsai are cultivars of species and sometimes the basic type itself is little known. The chief advantage of cuttings is that they reproduce the precise characteristics of the chosen plant.

All cuttings are taken from vigorous material. With either major type – hard cuttings (wood from prior season growth) or soft cuttings (current season growth) just firm at the base – the constant rule is always to take the most robust material available; forget weak material.

Generally, conifers may best be propagated from hard cuttings, and deciduous species from soft cuttings. Where ideal conditions are provided, the optimum seasons of winter for hard and summer for soft material may be broadened. In Surrey for example, it is possible to root Pines from December to May and Maples from March till June. The trick with Maples – particularly Yatsubusa variants – is to take the cutting early, thus enabling the rooted and potted-on plant to grow for a month or two on its new roots before the dormant period. This is the key to over-wintering Maples, together with total old leaf removal and good ventilation. Maple cuttings taken later, are very prone to collapse when the spring growth surge takes all the stored plant energy; the root system is too embryonic to function adequately. Happily, most other Bonsai subjects are not as demanding. All should be kept frost free in their first winter.

All cuttings need a ventilated, rooting medium firm enough for physical support. Man-made products should be *inert* and if incorporated, obtain confirmation before use. The sharp sands traditionally used in the UK are excellent but must be sieved and the really fine matter discarded. The coarsest grit is used for drainage and the medium-sized particles, mixed either with peat or vermiculite, make up the insertion medium.

Shallow seed trays with ample drainage holes make good insertion boxes. The cheap black plastic type are ideal. Fill each to heaping level, tap it to settle the medium and pack it lightly in after levelling. Stand each box in water with the level to the brim and wait till the water rises through the holes to the surface of the mixture (Fig. 37a). Remove boxes, drain, and cant to remove the surplus. Never compress after watering.

Cutting material is finally prepared for insertion now. Average cutting lengths are 7.5–10 cm (3–4 in). Working from the base, remove all foliage along one-half to two-thirds the total length of the cutting (Fig. 37b). Any floppy, apical material is pinched off (it only collapses and leads to mildew otherwise, in the case of deciduous species) and the cuttings are counted to allocate numbers per box. Using looped elastic, mark a nail at half the depth measured to serve as holemaker/depth gauge. It is important cuttings do not touch the bottom of the tray and they should be at least 5 cm (2 in) from the wall of the tray. Bitter experience teaches the value of these points. Prepare the holes by rank and file.

The base of each cutting is re-cut (Fig. 37f) using sharp, sterile scissors. Sterilize scissors with methyl alcohol. In Bonsai the propagator is concerned with aspects beyond the simple rooting process and therefore the type of cut

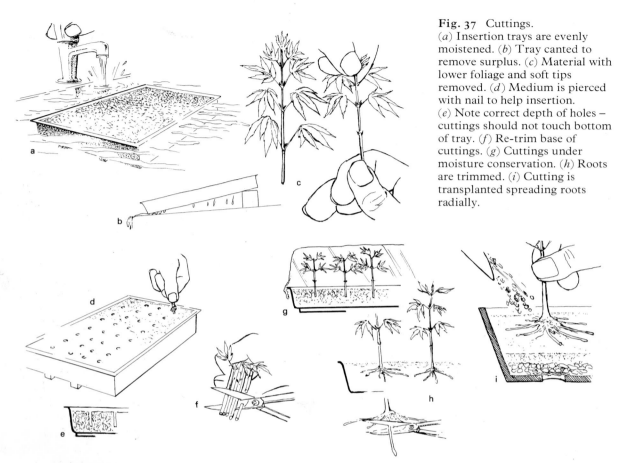

**Fig. 37** Cuttings. (*a*) Insertion trays are evenly moistened. (*b*) Tray canted to remove surplus. (*c*) Material with lower foliage and soft tips removed. (*d*) Medium is pierced with nail to help insertion. (*e*) Note correct depth of holes – cuttings should not touch bottom of tray. (*f*) Re-trim base of cuttings. (*g*) Cuttings under moisture conservation. (*h*) Roots are trimmed. (*i*) Cutting is transplanted spreading roots radially.

may be chosen for its effect when combined with the appropriate hormone strength in determining the type of root pattern generated. The slanting cut is akin to the traditional 'heel' cutting and normally produces a rather one-sided root pattern when combined with the normal mild-strength rooting hormone. The wedge cut where the base of the cutting is trimmed to a 'V' produces more evenly distributed roots and this initiation works best where medium to strong hormone levels are employed. The square cut, where high strength hormone is employed, will produce a football callus that leads to 360° of root initials but tissue may be damaged where maturity is not sufficient or if the hormone dip is of too great a duration.

It is a question of careful observation and experiment to find the means that produces the best distributed system. For *most* subjects the wedge cut combined with medium strength hormone will produce an evenly rooted plant. The freshly cut bases are dipped in the hormone preparation and inserted immediately in the prepared holes. When the box is complete firm cuttings down gently with the fingers and water the box again, draining off the surplus.

The cutting now requires constant maintenance of its water content until supplied with root. This means a humidifier must be provided but the medium must remain moist not soggy and the air must circulate but remain damp (Fig. 37*g*). Cover with a clear polythene lid that gives the cuttings comfortable head room. A wire frame with the plastic stretched across and taped works well. The cover is removed and the foliage is misted twice daily. The box is placed out of direct sun and draughts and the lid is propped open a little way. After 48 hours the cuttings are sprayed with a systemic fungicide which is repeated fortnightly. Soft, mid-summer cuttings take in about three to four weeks, but hard cuttings need longer – up to eight weeks or more – and may be helped by the introduction of bottom heat.

When the cuttings start to sprout and look perky, try a *gentle* test pull: if there is reasonable resistance, rooting has normally taken place. When certain, feed weekly for the next four weeks and then transplant with caution; newly formed roots are incredibly delicate and an entire system will come away if treated roughly. Prepare individual containers unless destined for group work. The soil must be open and light. A good mixture will be equal parts of leaf mould, peat, pine needle (rotted) and grit. This mixture cannot possibly compact and the embryo root system will expand rapidly through it. Plastic bag pots are useful for growing on and are very cheap. Half fill each one.

Even the root system by pruning (Fig. 37*h*) with sharp, sterilized scissors. Reduce heavy roots and prune any potential tap root, recognizable by its strong growth. Spread the root system as radially (Fig. 37*i*) as possible – young as it is, a good cutting should sit upright by itself. Gently add further soil, supporting the tree with the other hand so that it cannot shift and disarrange the roots. Top up and level off. Water in and after a month in partial shade, give feed weekly. Periodic foliage misting is still a good idea when one remembers.

Cuttings offer the opportunity to work with material already possessing mature characteristics – flowering cycles for instance are assured. Brittle subjects such as Quince and Firethorn may be pre-trained prior to separation for cuttings. Our nursery currently has both Quince and Firethorn that were trained as Spring shoots on the stock plant and inserted and wired into the trays. They were wire set and rooted almost simultaneously and are now transplanted and growing happily. It

is standard practice for most species to allow an establishment season or two where good feeding and watering can build the plant prior to training.

## Seedlings

Assuming one has obtained sound, viable seed ready for planting one will need a finer particled edition of the soil recommended for cuttings and more plastic trays. Soil particles should be around 3 mm ($\frac{1}{8}$ in) in size, this size structure will drain well without sinking. If necessary, put crocking discs over the drainage holes and prepare seed trays by filling seven eighths full with sieved compost. Tap the side of the tray to settle the soil and add more if necessary and plant the seeds. Tree seeds are normally lightly pressed in to half cover them, a very thin layer of compost is sifted over, levelled and then watered in well.

The trays are placed out of direct sun and water is withheld until the compost begins to lighten, indicating dryness. The trays should be evenly *damp* – sogginess leads immediately to rot problems. With difficult seeds such as Japanese Maple, it is a good thing to plant seed in the autumn so trays may be exposed to frost that will break seed dormancy naturally. With easier species keep the trays frost free. Shade is a useful factor at the beginning.

After seedlings germinate, treat immediately with systemic fungicide and repeat fortnightly. Ventilation and even soil dampness, combined with the prophylactic spray, control damp-off and other wilt conditions.

Seedlings must be left undisturbed for a season after germination. Sensible watering/feeding/fungicidal spraying programmes are faithfully followed, and are applicable from early March to August. During year 2, strong seedlings are transplanted and grown on for a year prior to training. Weaker seedlings are left undisturbed for another year.

## Layering

This is a very simple process and a way of securing material with an appreciable trunk that may be pre-shaped to taste. As with cuttings, the layering has all the inbuilt adult

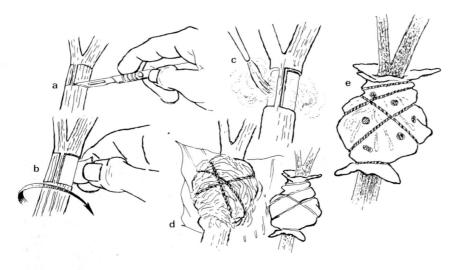

**Fig. 38** Layering: Aerial layer.
(*a*) Cut through bark with scalpel. (*b*) Remove flap.
(*c*) Dust with hormone.
(*d*) Wrap with wet sphagnum moss. (*e*) Wrap with polythene and, when root tips show, puncture the polythene to prevent rot. (*f*) *Gently* remove moss. (*g*) The layer is potted in a deep container with the roots spread radially.

characteristics but pre-shaping can be carried to a very advanced stage before separation. This process has the added attraction of being feasible anywhere, whether in Japan on specially planted stock trees, or back home in the hedgerow. Established hedges often featuring Hornbeam, Beech or Yew, can provide superb Bonsai. Hawthorn and Field Maple also respond well but be careful with Elm suckers for obvious reasons. I have been referring here to aerial layering; ground layering, or inarching, also produces excellent material.

## AERIAL LAYERING
Using a surgical scalpel or similar instrument, make two cuts ringing the limb to the heart-wood. The cuts are parallel and at right angles to the limb and may entirely girdle the trunk, or fall short, so a bridge 3 mm ($\frac{1}{8}$ in) wide is preserved. If the bridge is desired, make two parallel cuts along the limb ensuring the initial ring cuts meet them neatly. Then, preserving the bridge if chosen, remove the bark between the rings by peeling cleanly (Fig. 38*a*–*b*). The normal length of peeled area will be about 2.5–5 cm (1–2 in) so this is the distance between rings. Slower rooting subjects such as Pines, usually have the bridge retained. Subjects that root and form calluses quickly such as Maples and Apples will 'jump' the wound area and heal it without rooting, so they require entire ringing.

**Colour Plate 37.** Left: Formal Upright style Meyer's Juniper. 15 years. From nursery stock.
**Colour Plate 38.** Below: Formal Upright style Japanese Cedar. 40 years.

**Colour Plate 39.** Top left: Bark detail 50 year old Pine.

**Colour Plate 40.** Top right: Jin detail on Needle Juniper.

**Colour Plate 41.** Centre left: Bark detail 200-year old Pine.

**Colour Plate 42.** Above: Mame or small size Bonsai. 5 years.

**Colour Plate 43.** Left: Group style Japanese Larch. 12 years. Spring 1981.

Facing page

**Colour Plate 44.** Top left: Root Connected style Kyohime Maple. 25 years.

**Colour Plate 45.** Top right: Spring 1985.

**Colour Plate 46.** Bottom: Group style Japanese Larch Spring 1986.

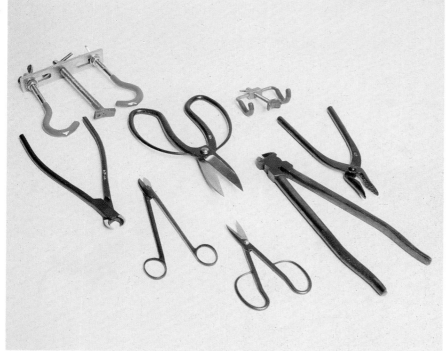

**Colour Plate 47.** Top: Mame or small size Bonsai pots.

**Colour Plate 48.** Above: Bonsai tools. *From top left, clockwise:* medium-size clamp, general purpose shears, small clamp, Jin pliers, large-size wire cutters, fine pruning scissors, long-handled scissors, and branch cutters.

If a multi-trunk variant or clump is desired, create the peeled area close to a branch whorl so the roots which appear directly from the edge of the upper ring, will develop in the immediate vicinity of the fork bases, initiating trunk flare. The peeled area is immediately dusted with rooting powder and wrapped in damp sphagnum moss which is secured with twine or raffia. This takes approximately two handfuls of moss, previously saturated with water and then wrung out. Clear polythene is wrapped around the moss, secured first below the lower ring and brought up to be secured again, in close contact, against the moss above the upper ring (Fig. 38c–d). Check monthly for dampness by opening the top tie. When first odd root ends appear, make sure the system is well ventilated by puncturing (Fig. 38c) the polythene five or six times – this makes for even rooting and protects long roots from die-back before separation.

When root tips appear fairly generally distributed, the layering may be separated. Sever the layered area and remove the polythene. A gentle probing usually brings the outer sphagnum away, but great care (Fig. 38f) should be taken when handling the new roots – they are as brittle as those of cuttings and so if the moss remains close to the trunk, leave it!

Prepare a temporary container half filled with the open soil mix. Infinitely gently, spread the new roots as radially as possible (Fig. 38g) and hold the layering so that it cannot move while filling the container to the brim with more soil. Tie the layering into the container with strings wrapped around the trunk and taken around the pot on every side. Water in well – soil first – and aftercare is standard.

GROUND LAYERING
This is the familiar process of pegging base shoots or lower branches to induce rooting. Pre-training is still possible and desirable, simply allow enough span of limb so the treated area can rise clear of the soil. The shoot or branch is gently bent down to check where it reaches the soil, do not release it once bent – place a stone on it till ready to work. Remove a large flap of bark on the underside (Fig. 39a–b), about half to two thirds the circumference and make the cuts with the

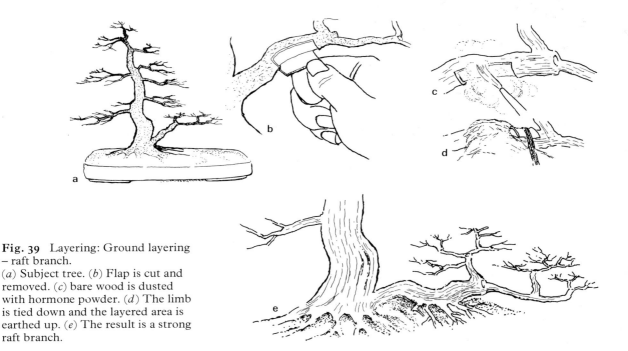

**Fig. 39** Layering: Ground layering – raft branch.
(a) Subject tree. (b) Flap is cut and removed. (c) bare wood is dusted with hormone powder. (d) The limb is tied down and the layered area is earthed up. (e) The result is a strong raft branch.

scalpel as for air layering. Immediately dust the peeled area with hormone powder and peg it down to the soil surface, using a wooden stake form like a tent peg (Fig. 39c–d).

The soil beneath can be varied according to choice. If in the garden and the soil is hard, it can be broken with a trowel and some potting mixture worked into it. Sometimes the stock plant can be an established Bonsai with redundant branches, in which case the main pot may be ringed with enough pots to take all the redundant limbs. Sometimes it is desired to transform a low, strong Bonsai branch into an attached Raft branch, in which case the standard method is followed being careful not to harm the parent Bonsai roots. The Raft branch is left attached and the newly rooted system gradually uncovered to feature the powerful new limb.

The soil above the pegged area is now added, heaped and contoured, pressing lightly to hold the shape when watered. The average ground layering needs mounding to about 7.5–10 cm (3–4 in) to allow for settlement. Water well, but gently.

Both methods of layering work best if carried out in spring, taking bud activity as the guide. Deciduous subjects normally root comfortably inside a season but some conifers can take two or more seasons. There are other layering techniques but for most normal situations these two should suffice.

## Grafting

This is a method to use when only tiny pieces of choice material, known not to root and impossible to layer, become available. In Bonsai, unless the graft is so low as to be covered with soil or disguised with root junctions, or if higher, unless perfectly healed and colour matched, the tree is considered inferior. Even when invisible or perfectly knit, Japanese purists regard it as two trees and therefore inferior. However it remains a good method to use in raising Pines for instance, and in fact the Japanese graft most of their Yatsubusa Pines.

The grafting process is not difficult as such, but success depends on a lot of factors which require careful provision and orchestration. The two elements are the scion material, or top piece to be propagated – this should be vigorous, dormant and no more than two years old – and the stock, which should be of a compatible species of the same age, vigour and thickness, but which should be commencing growth. With Pines, the scion material may be removed from the stock plant in December, when dormant, and if kept damp, will store till grafting time in January or February. The scions are bundled together with elastic bands, wrapped in paper kitchen towel, dunked in water, drained, then wrapped in polythene and kept in the fridge at no lower than 4.5° C (40° F). The potted Pine stocks are given warmth over the same period so they are breaking dormancy at grafting time.

At grafting time, scions and stock are paired to match in diameter (Fig. 40a). Trim base needles away from scions. Using a scalpel, wedge-cut the scion base (Fig. 40b–c). Bend the stock over as low as possible and make an incision at an angle to a depth one-third of the stock diameter and of the same length as the scion wedge. Without delay place the wedge-cut scion base into the stock incision, flexing the stock to keep it open, and align the bark on both exactly (Fig. 40d–f). Take the time to ensure a perfect fit. Release the stock gently and the returning limb should hold the scion in place. Wrap and tie the graft in position with soft polythene or elastic bands and paint the whole wound area with tree wound compound to seal it against the entry of air (Fig. 40g). The use of pliable wrapping prevents constriction.

The whole unit must be kept moist so the scion does not dehydrate, but at the same time, bottom heat will speed up the graft. A clear moistened polythene bag placed over the whole unit and then sealed will suffice. Bottom heat should be about 21° C (70° F). Ventilate the graft and re-seal the moisturizing bag every one to two days. Intermittent mist and bottom heat in a greenhouse or even a jam jar placed over the unit are other possibilities.

The graft has taken when new bud growth on the scion declares itself and it is then fed

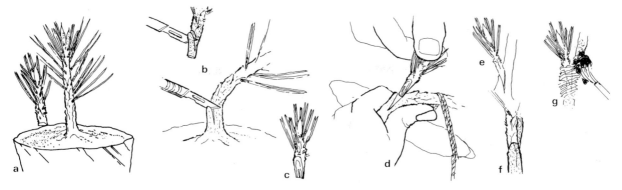

**Fig. 40** Grafting.
(*a*) Scion and stock are diameter matched. (*b*) Scion and stock are cut. (*c*) The scion wedge should be exactly the same length as the stock incision. (*d*) Insertion of scion. (*e*) Scion in position. (*f*) Bark in alignment. (*g*) Scion tied and painted.

**Plate 22**  Good graft created by careful caliper and bark matching. Yatsubusa Scots Pine on to Scots Pine stock.

**Plate 23**  Bad graft caused by disproportionate size of scion and stock, impossible to disguise in a high graft. Pumila Pine on to Scots Pine stock.

fortnightly till September. The stock may be pruned back, retaining some buds and needles, after three to four months and if all goes well, removed entirely close above the graft union in August of year two. This is side grafting and its chief advantage is a blend line with careful matching of diameter and alignment that disguises the union very well. The stock incision as always is made as low as possible and to achieve this, one can un-pot the stock, the better to control the low cut. The process is then slightly different, the stock is firmly gripped and the incision made of the same length, penetration and angle, but the scalpel cut begins so low that it finishes right *on* the root line. *Then* the stock is bent for the first time to admit the scion and establishment is standard. The choice of which method

75

is largely determined by dexterity! It is important to spread the roots radially at all transplantings and to compensate for the angle created by grafting where desired. Japanese Black Pine and Scots Pine make the best stocks and are compatible with most Black Pine, Scots Pine and Five needle cultivars.

## Nursery stock

This offers the opportunity to choose an instant trunk and reference to the style applications will hopefully simplify selection and stimulate ideas.

Nursery stock also introduces another factor: that of size. Bonsai are usually divided into three sizes: small, up to 15 cm (6 in); medium, up to 45 cm (1½ ft); and large, up to 90 cm (3 ft). There is a micro-size, up to 5 cm (2 in) and occasionally larger trees are grown for display in very large rooms. Measurements are taken from root bole to foliage tip.

The perfect piece of material, which does exist, has a tapered trunk. From notes I made in 1962 I find for example that Sequoias have been known to check their growth on transplanting for five or six years. They simply increase in diameter at the bole and reach pyramidal dimensions for their size before the leader 'takes off'. This habit of Sequoia is useful to know for the would-be Chokkan grower. The branching habit of the tree lends itself to this style.

Sadly, such instances of natural taper in nursery stock are rare. However, remember most Bonsai have induced taper, brought about by pruning and realignment of an upper shoot, the process being repeated two or three times. Sympathetically handled, the wounds heal, callus and vanish. The cuts are all made at branch junctions, at a slant where possible, and from the rear. All three factors mask the process and promote an ultimately natural appearance. With Chokkan trees, replacement spurs are always trained vertically. Cryptomeria, Yew, Cedar, Cypress, Spruce, Chinese Juniper and other Juniper species, Swamp Cypress, Dawn Redwood and Larch may all be found. Older nurseries are the best place to look for specimens.

Practically all the other styles may be discovered in rudimentary form. There are other obvious cases where conversion is simple: Cascades from sprawling prostrate Juniper and Cotoneaster; Clumps from Yew; Informals from Japanese Maples and Groups, and from Beech and Hornbeam hedging material. A nursery crawl makes a good day out! Remember with other styles the same taper inducement technique can be used to change the trunk angle at every cut. Often, very deep pruning 'makes' a Bonsai.

Stock should be of good foliage colour in the growing season; in winter make allowances for winter colour on evergreens (often bronze or purple) and if unsure, feel the foliage – dead foliage is dehydrated and brittle. All branches and twigs should be firm and the bark plump and unwrinkled. Avoid stock that has discoloured foliage other than that described and extensive dieback. Both conditions indicate bad roots, strangled, dehydrated or mushy. Check for insects and pests, scale insect is common.

Pick the stock up in late Winter to early Spring and transplant it. Style the material by bulk limb reduction to emphasize the vital structures. Some basic wiring may be carried out at this time if the stock is vigorous. If the stock is neglected but of too fine a quality to leave, the best treatment is to prepare a vast temporary container half filled with the open mixture, and wash as much soil from the mass as necessary to spread the roots, then place, and pot up the tree. Horrors to be encountered are: burlap left when the plant was lifted, balled and then potted when it failed to sell immediately, thus matting with the outer roots and strangling the inner; the potted on plant so root bound as to have a continual spiral of root around the pot old enough to have mature bark and an internal feeble, dry and rotted mass. Treatment for both conditions consists of unscrambling the outer mass and trimming it back gently. Washing the old soil does simplify matters. Remove as much of the burlap as is safe and in both cases spread the roots radially as much as possible and add further soil to stabilize the plant.

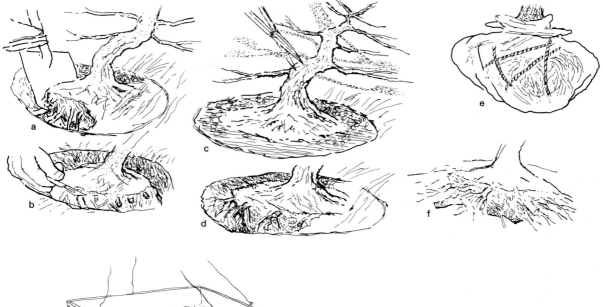

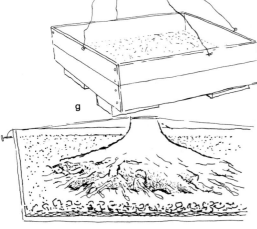

Fig. 41  Natural trees: collection.
(*a*) Chop around tree, excavate trench. (*b*) Reduce load
on root system by part shaping tree. (*c*) Fill trench
with soil mix. (*d*) After a year check for feeder roots.
(*e*) Ball the root system without disturbance.
(*f*) Examine root system at home. (*g*) Plant tree in
prepared box, placing the roots as radially as
possible.

Establishment period for vigorous stock is usually two months. For the weaker material, probably a year or more will be needed before secondary ciliary roots are strong enough for the tree to withstand wiring and pruning. Plants always declare their health by the state of their bud production, particularly Pines. Secondary wiring on established nursery stock may begin in year 2 if the tree is making a vigorous response, if it is not, delay *all* training for another season.

## Natural trees

Natural trees may be found virtually anywhere where there are factors to inhibit the complete performance of the tree. Some of the more likely sites in the UK have already been mentioned. For the location of promising sites and their caches of natural Bonsai one needs to have some knowledge of geology and meteorology. The problem is that both these factors are very local; Bonsai in the UK exist in really micro-climatic conditions. The important thing is first to obtain permission to dig and collect the trees.

### Method

1. In Spring, when bud activity begins, dig a 30–45 cm (1–1½ ft) diameter circle around the trunk, 30 cm (1 ft) deep (Fig. 41*a*).

Use a spade or trenching tool. Angle the chop outwards. Dig a second circle 7.5–15 cm (3–6 in) inside the first. This operation may also be done in August.

2. Excavate the soil between the circles to the same depth. Clean severed roots with a scalpel (Fig. 41b–c). Paint heavy cuts with tree paint. Clean wounds heal fast and feeder roots are triggered. Replace with open soil mixture.

3. Preserving the cone index and remembering the section on Styles, prune out redundant limbs and shorten the head and upper limbs according to the impression made by the tree. Limb reduction balances root reduction.

4. In a year's time, check for feeder roots in the trench (Fig. 41d). If present, undercut the trench in the outer circle. If the tree still holds, feel for the anchor roots and cut them with secateurs. Retain the soil – the feeder roots hold most of it anyway – ball the root in wet newspaper or sphagnum (Fig. 41e), then wrap in polythene and tie. An anti-desiccant or water misting should be given over the foliage.

5. At home, near the standard temporary container prepared prior to the trip, the roots are unwrapped and examined (Fig. 41f). If the fine roots are plentiful a Bonsai pot may be used but, if patience can stand it, use a temporary container. Gently unravel and spread the roots.

6. Place the tree in the half-filled container and place the roots as radially as possible (Fig. 41g). Add more soil while holding the tree till it is reasonably stable. Guy strings from nails in the container wall will hold the trunk steady. Cushion contact areas with rubber tubing or soft towelling. Old bark is visually precious and fragile.

7. Probe the soil in and around the root system with the fingers to eliminate air pockets. Take care not to compress the soil. Top up the container with more soil to just short of the rim (for watering) and level off neatly.

8. Carry the unit to a prepared shaded area, and place the container on bricks for extra ventilation and drainage. Wildlings are greatly helped if initially watered in with Vitamin $B_1$ transplant solution. This improves survival rate quite amazingly. Confine the use of solution to the soil. Spray foliage with straight water.

9. The tree is essentially a gigantic cutting, so treatment reflects this fact: water content is preserved by top spraying but roots are kept moist rather than wet. After their first saturation, maintain a careful watch for dryness. This normally takes at least a week, as the newly formed roots are not fully operational. Water when dry, but avoid sogginess at all times. A fortnightly fungicidal spray is a good idea.

10. Provided the top of the tree can be moistened whenever dry, for example by using mist, bottom heat will encourage rooting.

11. Often the tree will be trainable inside a year, but it is better to delay shaping the tree till it feels solid with root, when the trunk is *gently* rocked. Aftercare and subsequent training are standard.

# 3 Mechanics of Bonsai

## The development process

The tree as you will have gathered is the product of many techniques. Mechanical application does not in itself produce a classical Bonsai and many trees are ruined by this simplistic approach. Applied aesthetics in every aspect of the tree *combined* with sound basic techniques produce those magnetic images we all strive after. In creating Bonsai one has constantly to be aware of the property and dual nature of each technique in order to retain and develop the essential freshness of the design. The term 'applied aesthetics' therefore symbolizes both the distillation of beauty into programmable techniques and also the determination to mask horticultural effort so only the image remains.

There is obviously no such thing as a formula of beauty, the key is to master the techniques and awareness of all their functions so this knowledge is instantly available in response to the demands of inspiration. When totally absorbed, the techniques become the artist's handwriting and no longer constitute a block between idea and execution.

The purpose of any apparent formula in the book is simply as a finger post to indicate areas that deserve to become part of the handwriting but they are never considered an end in themselves.

### PRUNING

This is the means by which one limits the trunk and branch length, regulates the number of limbs, imposes form and change, tidies foliage texture, disposes of twigs and sub-branches, and all the while refining and adding nuances at every stroke.

SOFT PRUNING This is carried out with the fingers to induce denser growth which is neater in size. With a Maple for example (Fig. 42a–c), the pruning causes latent buds (carried in the leaf axils and down the limb) to shoot, thereby doubling the foliage weight. Duplication effectively halves nutritional activity at that point, therefore the secondary shoots are smaller.

It is possible to alter the shape of the limb by retaining the shoot pointing in a radically different but more pleasing direction: the opposing shoot is rubbed off. The result is a kinked branch with no wound tissue. These techniques are followed with most deciduous species.

Soft pruning is applied to foliage profiles of all species to improve density of foliage, and therefore peripheral twig weight. It also functions as a simple maintenance device and saves trained contours from becoming ragged.

Trees with non-determinate resting buds, such as Cypress, Cryptomeria and Juniper, are tip pruned using the *fleshy* part of the thumb and fore-finger (Fig. 42d–f). This finer point ensures the shoot is the ideal length for removal. Secondary shoots follow and these are tipped and followed by tertiary shoots and so on.

Trees with well defined resting buds such as Pine (Fig. 42g) and Spruce, are also soft pruned. The new Pine shoot is removed completely if extended to over 2.5 cm (1 in) and the other buds in the whorl are shortened back, retaining two or three sheaths of needles, just as the needles break through the wall of the Pine shoot. Spruce shoots are removed with thumb and fore-finger when long enough

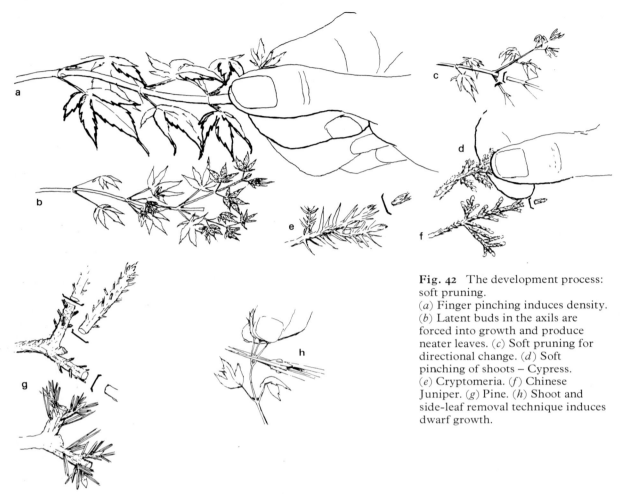

**Fig. 42** The development process: soft pruning.
(*a*) Finger pinching induces density. (*b*) Latent buds in the axils are forced into growth and produce neater leaves. (*c*) Soft pruning for directional change. (*d*) Soft pinching of shoots – Cypress. (*e*) Cryptomeria. (*f*) Chinese Juniper. (*g*) Pine. (*h*) Shoot and side-leaf removal technique induces dwarf growth.

– these are twisted off. Spruce *normally* flush only once a season and Pines, once to twice a season.

Leaf cutting, the technique used to reduce foliage size, is best confined to Trident Maple, Elm and Zelkova. On healthy trees, when foliage hardens, cut the leaves off but retain the stalk or petiole. The process is preceded and followed by a sound feeding programme after the secondary flush of leaves. Avoid leaf stripping any weak areas on the tree.

The removal of shoot and side-leaves (Fig. 42*h*) as commented on, is the alternative technique to leaf cutting and one which is nowhere near as injurious. It is practised throughout the season and thus puts far less strain on the plant.

The technique is to remove the terminal shoot and adjacent pair of leaves, whenever and wherever larger leaves appear. Secondary foliage is compact and locally produced, enabling one to keep leaf size balanced without harm. Sound feeding must of course accompany the technique. The Raft Trident Maple illustrated (on p. 57), has been treated in this way for the past seven years. There is a tendency for the dwarfing effect to carry over from season to season. Soft pruning is ideal because it leaves no scars.

HARD PRUNING This pruning is executed with scissors that vary from those used in needlework to enormous pincers like bolt cutters (see p. 150). Major surgery on conifers can nearly always be disguised, by using the Jin technique, to convert the redundant limb to an element often more cogent to the design than when living.

The biggest cuts are made when a trunk is being formed and normally effect an angular change and initiate the programme of induced taper. However, most hard pruning is confined to the branches for taper inducement, leading also to the same type of angular changes. Branches may be roughly divided into three areas; the first section, from trunk to one-third along being the most simple. This section states the angle of the limb and features the most dynamic of any curves used. The middle section displays less curvature of the main limb and is often itself divided, the secondary branches springing from this area and dividing at least twice. The peripheral section is a diffusely linear area where sub-branches ramify and terminate in the finest of twigs.

Monitoring the amount of growth extension by cutting back is best done in spring, summer and autumn. August is the best month for 'autumn' pruning which relieves the tree of some of the extra load thereby reducing natural dieback. It should be stressed at this point that all pruning works best when the tree is in good health – a well fed tree is very responsive.

Heavy feeding stimulates long, heavy shoots. With hard pruning such shoots become ideal emergent branch material.

The following is a suggested outline programme found to work well on most deciduous subjects, but modified for Zelkova, where limbs are not wire-curved, but straightened. Broad-leaved evergreens such as Azaleas also respond well. Coniferous subjects may, to a more limited degree, be developed in this way, but accurate knowledge of potential budding habits and precise judgement in feeding are necessary to avoid enfeebled, or equally, over-coarse responses.

It is a matter of individual experience and meticulous note-keeping. Pines for example, under ideal conditions, will produce up to nine breaks of bud in a season. This was recorded during 1975 in Surrey. The proliferation implications are obvious, but refining the result is tricky.

As shoots develop, the central shoot extends and produces lateral pairs of leaves each carrying latent buds. These budded leaf junctions are known as nodes and the intervals between, along the shoot, as internodal lengths. Heavy feeding produces one or two short, basal, internodal lengths per shoot and subsequent intervals rapidly increase in length. When the extending shoot has reached four to five pairs of leaves, its diameter should be around 3 mm ($\frac{1}{8}$ in) and this is an ideal thickness for wire shaping. If this diameter is produced earlier, wire immediately (Fig. 43a–b). Shaping with covered wire combats the straight horizontal or vertical appearance. It is only necessary to curve the vital first internodal section. Coil loosely, this avoids constriction. The shoot is now permitted to rocket and make several feet in length. Rapid extension means rapid diameter increase and the newly wired form will be set very quickly; Maple and Elm limbs may exceed 6 mm ($\frac{1}{4}$ in) in diameter and be set inside a month. The loosely coiled wire is removed, cut off if necessary (Fig. 43c), and the curved, basal section pruned back to the first or second (short node) pair of leaves (Fig. 43d).

Such hard pruning carried out at a period of strong activity provokes an eruption of buds. The best positioned of these are retained and the cycle is repeated, curving the limb in a contra-relative direction. This technique will result in an elegantly curved, feminine branch.

A more varied and forceful branch can be built by leaving every other extending basal internode unwired and straight – relying in this case on change of direction (obtained by bud choice) for character. The combination of curves and angularities is pleasing and convincing (Fig. 43e–f).

Such forcing techniques, accompanied by additional feed, are begun at signs of bud activity and continue till June. After June, reduce feeding by half and revert to soft pruning with the fingers, and by the end of the

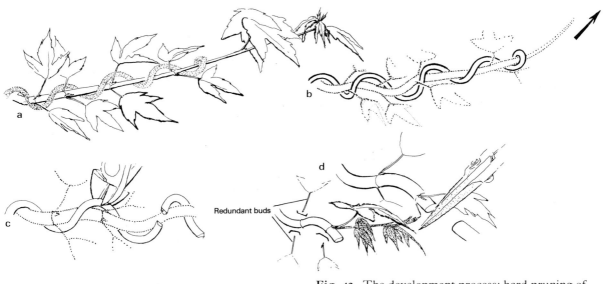

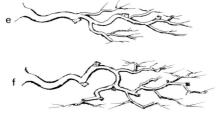

Redundant buds

**Fig. 43** The development process: hard pruning of branches.
(*a*)–(*b*) The extending shoot is allowed 4–5 pairs of leaves before being wire shaped. (*c*) Wire is removed after rapid growth has increased diameter and made wires snug. Delay leads to constriction. (*d*) Curved basal section is pruned back and redundant buds are removed. (*e*) Branch pattern created by repeating curve/prune cycle. (*f*) Branch pattern created by repeating curve/prune/straight cycle.

season one should be rewarded with the sight of autumn branches with character, taper, and nicely spurred side branches.

The amount of growth extension permitted annually, is determined by sentiment, ruthlessness and patience. It is a hard thing to sacrifice branch length, when to finish a tree another 30 cm (1 ft) is needed in every direction. But, if the extension is no more than 5 cm (2 in) a year, which should be the case if the suggested techniques are followed – when the branches *do* make their length, what a visual feast!

The same techniques, without heavy feeding in this instance, are followed on all side-branches and secondary and tertiary twigs. Remember always to encourage diameter so the shoot does not die back when wired.

So far pruning has been seen as the regulator of positive areas. But it can also be used as the creator of space inside crowded areas. This method of pruning reinforces the image by trimming back and thinning, it is grooming in fact (Fig. 44), taken to a highly developed

level. Hopefully, the comments made in the chapter on Style Development will have made desirable branch patterns clear. It is the function of grooming to emphasize underlines by judicious foliage removal, to remove redundant, overly dense or dead twigs, and to adjust, regulate and shape the vital, interrelative negative areas thus assisting the health and vigour of the tree by admitting extra light and air and by redirecting apical vigour. Grooming is in fact, a useful process!

Branch lines of all species should be checked at least twice a year for basal growth, also remove any that threaten trained branches by ugliness or competition. Hanging foliage is particularly irritating and tends to diminish the visual scale of the branch.

Pines and species where foliage is erectly borne or arranged to do so, should have older, lower foliage removed. If too much needle growth is removed from Pines it inhibits or prevents adventitious budding, so be cautious. Needle Junipers and others should be purged of dead leaves, which clog branches,

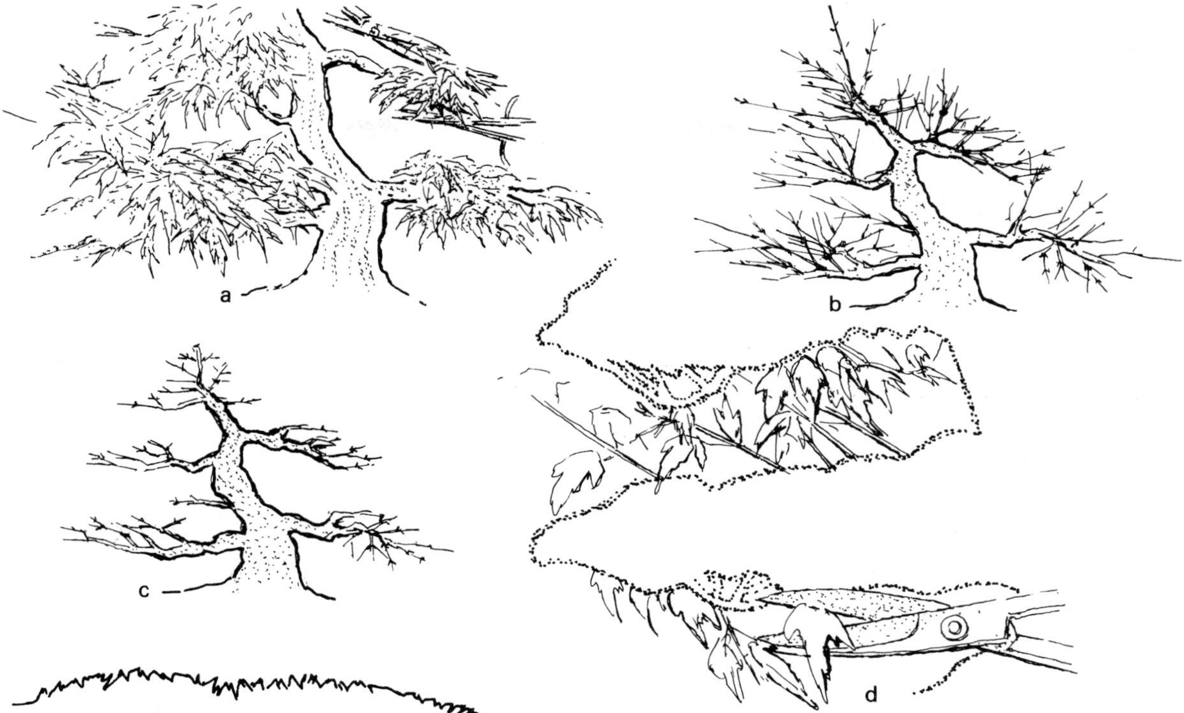

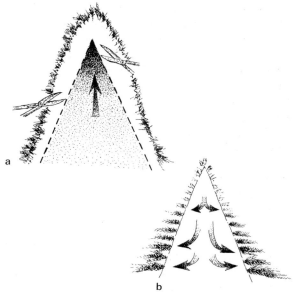

Fig. 44  The development process: grooming.
(*a*) Overall view of tree as grooming commences.
(*b*) Underlying twig pattern before grooming.
(*c*) Underlying twig pattern after grooming.
(*d*) Shaping and regulating negative areas. (*e*) Purging dead and older portions of evergreen foliage.

Fig. 45 (*below*)  The development process: index of vigour.
(*a*) The cone of vigour. (*b*) Redirecting apical dominance.

spoil their appearance and impair their health. The branches of all evergreens benefit from cleansing. Profiles are also checked for wayward shoots which are removed or wired to keep the line. If close pruning is done in the early season, budding is compact and tends to remain so for a long period. Equally predictably, pruning in mid-season sparks off rank growth.

All pruning, at any time, no matter what the object, *must* be subordinate to the index of vigour – conical in force and present in every tree (Fig. 45*a*). The force is at its greatest concentration in the narrow apex and least in the lower, spreading branches where one needs the heaviest weight! It follows therefore that pruning through the upper reaches and apical region, is harder and deeper than that practised down below, and the scale of se-

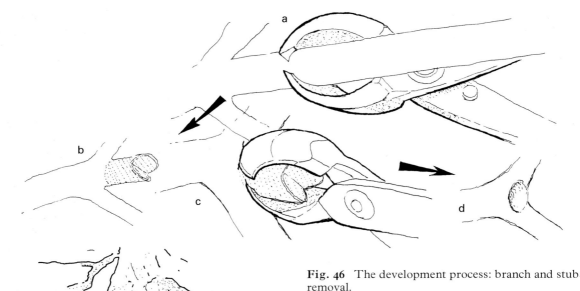

**Fig. 46** The development process: branch and stub removal.
(*a*) Heavy cuts are made initially with side cutters.
(*b*) A stub is left; note concave cut. (*c*) The stub is removed after die-back using Wen cutters.
(*d*) Dimpled depression is left which heals rapidly.
(*e*) Heavy front branch removal. The wound is hollowed out – known as Uro.

verity is graduated and truly conical in form (Fig. 45*b*).

The greater spread of foliage in the lower region, therefore, affords an increase in trunk diameter where it is visually important, which in turn means an increase in the diameter of the lower trunk, thereby assisting taper. Knowledge therefore of the cone enables one to reverse the natural polarity of the tree and to exploit the diffused result. Unattended trees rapidly assert apical dominance so pruning and lightening of the upper tree is vital.

Cuts caused by hard pruning are treated in different ways according to the age of the specimen, species and size of wound. Cuts of up to 3 mm ($\frac{1}{8}$ in) are not usually treated unless made during the August trimming when all wounds are treated with bituminous paint.

Cuts up to finger thick made in taper inducement where the old limb or vestige of it is not a candidate for Jin, are removed with side cutters, which create a concave cut. Cuts are made leaving a stub (Fig. 46*a*). The stub dies back naturally and can be removed later using Wen cutters (cutters with egg-sectioned jaws) that leave a shallow, dimpled concavity (Fig. 46*b–d*). If the initial cut is too close, die-back can occur and take either fork with it, so the stub is a natural barrier. Heavy trunk pruning is best done in autumn and winter protection is imperative. *Any* trees subjected to heavy pruning must be shielded from frost.

Heavy trunks are cut leaving stubs and it is the secondary removal after die-back that leaves the area clean. Once again, factors of Jin conversion or total removal dictate the treatment. Use a saw to make the initial upper and lower cuts just as trees are pruned in the garden. The stub is dabbed with wound paint if a little too close, otherwise it is allowed to dry. For the secondary clean-up use side cutters, Wen cutters and a scalpel if necessary to clean and pare the bark flat for good healing. The wound is then painted. Most larger wounds on deciduous species are best left flat or slightly hollow to promote callus, certainly if they occur in forks. Wounds caused by the removal of heavy branches in full view from the front of the tree, can be hollowed out to good advantage, creating a woodpecker hole. Such a trunk hollow is very natural looking and is called Uro (Fig. 46e).

WIRING

This is the positive way of placing and shaping a limb so a design becomes precisely as conceived in terms of posture. It is not in itself a complete answer but is a tool to be known and used with the others. By coiling and bending, complete changes of direction are possible, as are smaller movements and detailed work often of great subtlety.

Wire training involves selecting malleable wire stout enough to hold the reshaped area in position; the wire is first locked, by securing it around an adjacent limb when branch training, or by thrusting it between the roots when trunk shaping. The wire is coiled so it is just in contact with the bark, allowing surplus wire to project for extension training. The limb is then bent, by placing thumbs at the concavity and fingers on the convexity to be formed and finally, very gently forming the shape.

Established three-year-old material is easily wire shaped by coiling. The trunks of such young stock are stout enough to resist injury but thin enough to be minutely refined. The trunk form is established first according to the chosen style and branches are shaped later as already discussed. The wire chosen should be of sufficient strength to just hold the trunk. Flexing the limb and matching the resistance with wire of appropriate gauge is the easy way to choose; wiring is basically a finger skill.

Young stock and some older plants do not like bare metal. It is sensible to use plastic-sheathed wire, or to resort to wrapping wires with paper tape in the traditional way. Having selected the wire (two or three may be coiled in parallel if necessary to hold) cut it so it is 15 cm (6 in) longer than the trunk and insert it in between the roots, close in to the trunk and to a good depth. This is the anchor point and must not shift or leverage is negated. Very gently, coil the wire in a upward spiral making bark contact. On a trunk of 30 cm (12 in) the coils should be about 2 cm ($\frac{3}{4}$ in) apart. Latent buds or embryo branches are featured on outer bends and wire coils passing adjacent to planned convexities make precise bending more positive.

The standard style for most trunk shaping is the Informal Upright, which is accomplished quite easily by curving the trunk either left or right to the first outer bud and then curving back in contra-relation to the second bud and so on. The result will be as flat as a capital 'S'. Bonsai trunks need depth. Having established the two-dimensional 'S', check that secondary, and tertiary bends and so on diminish rapidly in size. Then bend the first curved section backwards and the second section forwards; the third section is taken back and the final section is raked really sharply forward (Fig. 47a–d). The resulting form will have depth no matter how crude and corrective minor adjustments are made at this point.

Never remake any major bends, especially when acute. Trees have cells that when wired are compressed in the concavity and severely stressed over each convexity. Dramatic changes usually rip both and the tree is crippled and dies. When after a month or two the cells are realigned the tree will adopt the imposed shape and appear quite natural. It is important to check trunk wires for constriction, wires 'bite' when the tree fattens, so always loosen any that appear tight.

When wiring, always watch for cracks appearing in the bark on convexities and listen for creaks at the same points. If either are noticed, that area has had enough; wire no

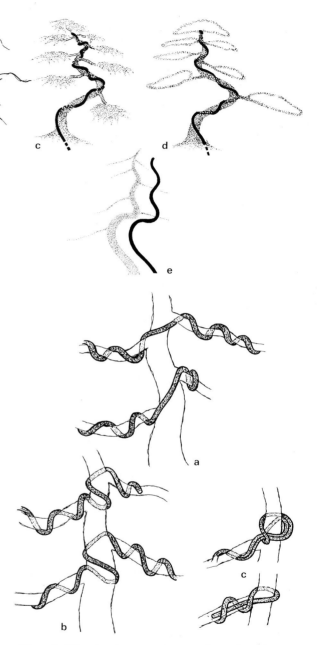

**Fig. 47** The development process: trunk wiring.
(*a*) The trunk is coiled securing the base in the soil.
(*b*) Fingers and thumbs are placed as shown and trunk is bent gently. (*c*) Side view of typical Informal Upright styled from a cutting. Note forward tilt at the half-way point. (*d*) Front view. Note branches issuing from trunk convexities. (*e*) Wire former for shaping light trunks.

further. If a trunk is snapped through wiring it can generally be saved providing the bark down one side of the break is entire. Simply slap a good covering of wound seal paint over the area to keep the air out and move the tree to a protected area. All freshly wired trees need a rest for at least a month and protection and feeding are a good idea. No heavy pruning demands are made on the tree. Trees usually have their branches developed in the manner described under 'hard pruning' beginning in the second year. Older trees from nursery stock and natural material may have trunk and branches trained in the same year *if* they are strong. It is safer to rest the plant between trunk and branch sessions.

Branch training (Fig. 48) begins with matching wire and resistance again. Anchor the wire by passing it round the base of a neighbouring branch, ensuring the wire is at least 15 cm (6 in) longer than the limb. Coil the limb and bend it to the motif chosen for the specimen, remembering that flat, multi-curving, convex or concave section bases (Fig. 49) all have their place, but the theme once decided, has to be thoroughly explored and exploited. Introduction of a different motif

**Fig. 48** The development process: branch wiring.
(*a*) Incorrect wiring. Badly located branch wires that do not give maximum bend.
(*b*) Correct wiring. Both limbs are effectively controlled as the wire is close in to the trunk and adjacent to the primary bends.
(*c*) Alternative branch wiring.

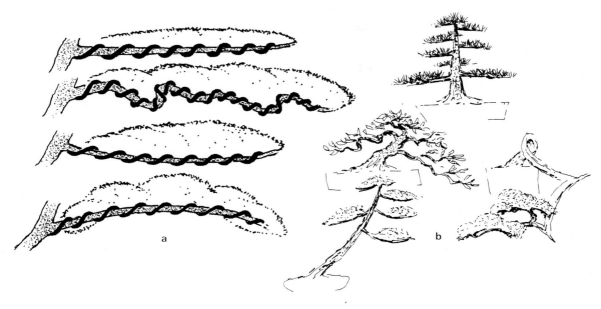

**Fig. 49**  The development process: branch bases.
(*a*) *from top*: straight, multi-curving, convex and concave branch bases. (*b*) Trees showing the four types.

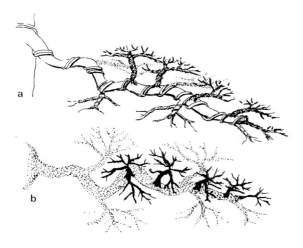

**Fig. 50**  The development process: establishment of branch profile.
(*a*) Side view. (*b*) Overhead view showing raised spine.

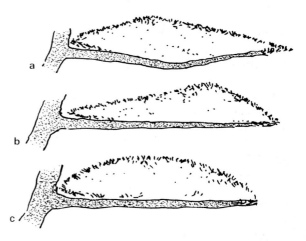

**Fig. 51**  The development process: branch profiles.
(*a*) Modified lozenge. (*b*) Triangular. (*c*) Dome.

breaks the logic of the design and destroys harmony – both of the tree and of the viewer – the offending branch will always obtrude.

Upper branches are established at the same time, first by wiring sub-branches outwards so they are flattened and observe the spine of the main branch. Tips of twigs are elevated

and these form the profile. Plan and side elevations have been discussed. The technique of establishing profile (Figs. 50 & 51) is very simple and consists merely of precise terminal placement, to create either the dome, triangle or whatever at its highest point and the peripheral shapes are three dimensionally

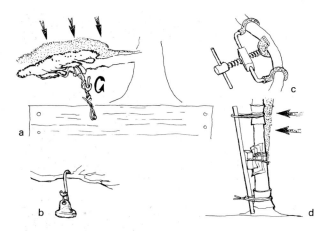

**Fig. 52** The development process.
(a) Suspended wiring. (b) The lead fishing weight, a rather random method of suspended wiring. (c) Light clamp. (d) Heavy metal former for straightening trunk.

Other devices used in wiring include clamps (Fig. 52c) of various types, the most versatile being those operating on a push-pull principle. These consist usually of a plate pierced three times, with flanking claws for the convex side, and with a centrally placed threaded push-pad for the concavity. The claws and pads simply operate in opposition and the bend is created one thread at a time. This is in fact not as Gothic a horror as it might appear and is far gentler in action than wire. Precise bends may be created in awkwardly located wood. The clamps are available in sizes from about 5 cm (2 in) up to 30 cm (1 ft) to cater for most trunk diameters. Other clamps are huge and operate more like jacks; these are designed for bending very large material and it takes expert care not to separate the bark with this pattern.

Often the object is to straighten, rather than bend a trunk and for this purpose heavy wire will often suffice. Another possibility is a heavy metal former with the trunk tied to it (Fig. 52d). Sometimes a cushioned pad between trunk and former is located to correct a bend where precise leverage is required. Leverage is obtained by tying securely above and below the pad. All friction areas must be cushioned prior to this operation.

Copper wire is most often used and is first toughened over gentle heat, five minutes in a bonfire or over a ball of newspaper is enough, overheating makes the copper brittle. There is nothing worse than having a major revelation and defunct wire simultaneously! Annealed copper wire always gives a good result and is quiet in appearance. Once annealed keep it dry, copper stiffens where it reabsorbs moisture. Copper is reclaimable and may be straightened.

Copper anodized aluminium wire is popular in Japan, the anodization prevents the pitting associated with aluminium and looks nicer. Uncoated malleable aluminium wire is alright, but it does obtrude. Aluminium is generally very pleasant to use and gives a positive result without mangling tree or fingers.

Plastic covered wire is excellent for young

achieved by splayed-out placement of their terminals. The tips form the desired contour and the splayed angle becomes shallower and eventually flat. The splayed height technique works well for all species and is used especially in the refinement of Pines where foliage peripheries need careful alignment.

Another wiring method that works well is that of suspended wiring (Fig. 52a–b). This is a simple technique where a limb is guyed down either to the trunk or to a wire looped around the container or similar. The technique is gentle but positive and where a temporary wooden container is used, very versatile, because all sorts of additional ties can be secured to the walls. Where friction areas occur they are protected with tubing or soft fabric. A turnbuckle in the guy line will give added control if desired. Refinements of great subtlety are possible when a profiled branch is guyed down because the posture is changed by induction. The newly distributed weight affects all other angles and therefore the dynamic balance is also affected, thus offering further possibilities.

Heavy wire formers may be used to shape young trees which are simply tied to them. This is not violent and may be used to shape trees that are known to hate wire, such as Cherries.

## FIBREGLASS ROCK CONSTRUCTION

Project: To fashion a rock with raised banks and a quartz river. This rock was featured at the International Bonsai Congress Convention in Minneapolis in 1987.

**Colour Plate 49.** Right: Initial chicken wire shape showing reinforcing strips.

**Colour Plate 50.** Below: Main contours positioned.

**Colour Plate 51.** Below right: Final wire contours added.

**Colour Plate 52.** Bottom: Big jump forward: fibreglass and mat completed. Strata modelling underway using exterior resin bond concrete.

**Colour Plate 53.** Right: Front view showing modelling.

**Colour Plate 54.** Below: Rear view.

**Colour Plate 55.** Below right: 'Wave' configuration. A river strata was added to simulate layered quartz.

**Colour Plate 56.** Bottom: The concrete is coated with clear resin as a sealer, then the whole is spray-painted with matt black.

**Colour Plate 57.** Left: Colouring underway. Note lower left area where stippled colour is being applied.
**Colour plate 58.** Below left: Authentication shot: real rock in foreground.
**Colour Plate 59.** Below: Close up.
**Colour Plate 60.** Bottom: Final view. The idea was to feature two tall Pines planted on the left bank. Wire loops were incorporated into the planting surface as location ties. Mosses and accent plants were added to naturalise everything using saikei techniques of bedding into peat/loam paste.

# BONSAI DISPLAY

**Colour Plate 61.** Right: The top deck under way. Materials used were high-density polystyrene blocks push-nailed together.
**Colour Plate 62.** Below: Varnished wood trim is being tacked on to finish the display in a manner recalling traditional Japanese Tokonomas.
**Colour Plate 63.** Below right: The general display on the stand during the show.
**Colour Plate 64.** Bottom: Gold! The author's hair needs pruning!

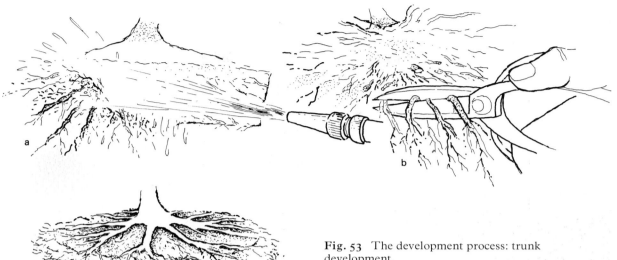

**Fig. 53** The development process: trunk development.
(*a*) Wash outer soil away. (*b*) Heavier, lower roots are pruned. (*c*) The tree is seated with the heavier, upper roots well spread.

stock, tender shoots, tying in roots, wire-sensitive subjects and for people like myself who own a lot of plants and face the danger of overlooking sober coloured wire. Galvanized wire is best confined to locating crocking discs.

Plants may be prepared for wiring by feeding well in the season prior to treatment and by easing back on watering a day or two before so the tissue is less sappy and brittle. Old trees resent, and are too weak to adopt, trunk realignment. If these must be restyled it is better to try pruning and postural changes.

Wire cutters of the type where blades meet right to the nose are a must. Aluminium wire is easily removed (remember to reverse the application process and take the strain in the fingers) because it remains soft. Copper is rock hard and it is more sensible to cut it away than risk years of work. Wire gauges 8 to 24 are used and of these, 12 to 22 are the most common.

TRUNK DEVELOPMENT

From seedling to giant, all trees rely on roots that are radially placed to ensure stability and their origins at the bole cause it to swell and produce the familiar flare line. The flare and buttress are the foundation of the trunk taper and these are programmed in good Bonsai training. As the trunk grows and diversifies, so a mirror development takes place in the roots, and therefore well spread roots create stability, buttress, flare, taper and well spread limbs. Equally, meagre or malformed roots are echoed with poor spread and faulty branches.

All potential Bonsai should have these desirable features and they must be established at the first transplanting. The establishment process involves spreading the entire root system and this entails washing the outer soil away so the roots may be unravelled (Fig. 53*a*). The lower roots, particularly heavy ones, are pruned hard (Fig. 53*b*) and the upper roots that will constitute the surfaced radials are spread and the tree is seated (Fig. 53*c*). With the surface roots spread, the bole should be stable. The surface roots are trimmed back, by about a third, spread again, as evenly as the spokes of a wheel, and enough soil is added to cover and anchor the roots.

Use a large temporary box or the open ground. If a box is used, ensure drainage is good and the soil is open. Soil capacity should be of generous volume and if open ground is

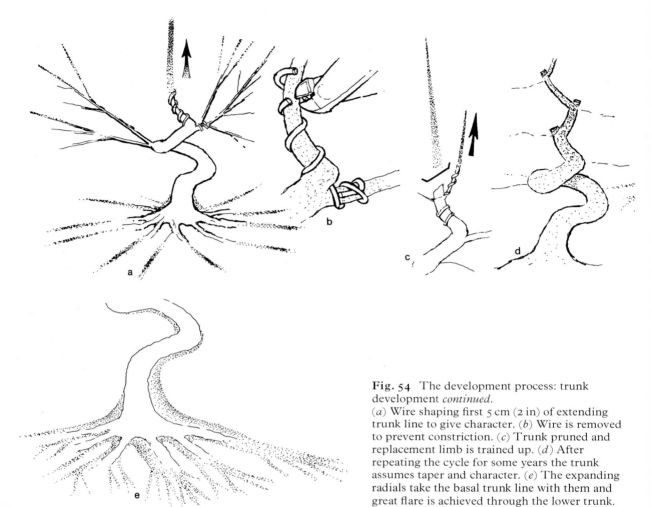

**Fig. 54** The development process: trunk development *continued*.
(*a*) Wire shaping first 5 cm (2 in) of extending trunk line to give character. (*b*) Wire is removed to prevent constriction. (*c*) Trunk pruned and replacement limb is trained up. (*d*) After repeating the cycle for some years the trunk assumes taper and character. (*e*) The expanding radials take the basal trunk line with them and great flare is achieved through the lower trunk.

used the area must be well broken up and the soil carefully structured using the open mixture. It is best to use pre-shaped, wire-free plants. Water in well. After the settling-in month, feeding is heavy. The technique is essentially the same as that suggested for branch building: it is vital to wire shape the first 5 cm (2 in) of extending trunk line (Fig. 54*a*), afterwards diameter increase overgrowths are pruned preserving the first or second nodes. Trunks should be pruned at least three times a season to encourage taper and character (Fig. 54*b–d*), unchecked trunks are columnar.

In the ground it is virtually impossible to refine branches and basic pruning is usually the best one can do. A box, being mobile, gives the chance to grow the tree at eye level and therefore branches can be built at the same time.

To supply all the energy needed, the tree needs weekly feed from March to June, when the amount is reduced by half to the end of July and half again through August. The length of overgrowth achieved before each pruning determines the diameter increase. Warmth and sound watering schedules are essential, but even using greenhouses, it is a sad fact that the UK is not really warm enough for the spectacular annual increases recorded in hot climates. The increases though are worthwhile and occasionally staggering. Following radial establishment, the increasing trunk weight is reflected and paced by root progression and this leads directly to rapid buttressing and flare (Fig. 54e). Diameter increases recorded in Surrey often show an initial leap from 3 mm ($\frac{1}{8}$ in) to 2.5 cm (1 in) in three months open growth but it is during year 2 that dramatic increase occurs.

In either state, the trees should be root pruned every third spring so they have two full seasons rampage per cycle. There are no limits to how long the tree can be developed by these methods, provided the lines are varied and tapered. If the tree threatens to become coarse it should be repotted into a Bonsai pot and grown slowly with continual pinching to re-establish finer structure. This is a simple matter when the roots are so well spread.

The roots themselves thicken when wet and assume bark if exposed to air, therefore keeping them covered and spread will give the maximum diameter and lead directly to flare at the bole. When uncovered, the power and beauty of such a system is breathtaking as the bark forms.

It must be stressed that these methods of inducing rapid growth should not be used on natural material or on stock of distinct character for any length of time – rapid growth thickens and coarsens and fine detail may be irretrievably lost. A limited spell of open growth however is a tonic for most root-bound nursery stock or established Bonsai that have been neglected.

The suggested rapid growth method has been used over ten years in Surrey, and others trying the method report equal success throughout the UK. It is important to consider it only as a pre-Bonsai technique where the structure is being built; Bonsai techniques proper begin in the pot.

REPOTTING AND SOIL
This is the all-vital process that ensures and concentrates vigour in the root through the removal of inactive aging portions. New feeder roots are stimulated close in around the trunk enabling the tree to thrive in a limited environment. As the roots flourish so the branches reflect their activity and bud profusely. Repotting/root pruning is carried out when the tree becomes rootbound and this condition is looked out for in the spring and if found, root pruning must not be delayed.

SOIL The condition and nature of the soil as already defined is ideal for most species. To reiterate: leaf mould, peat, rotted pine needle and grit in equal parts make an excellent mixture. If micro-climatic conditions tend to dry the trees and exposure cannot be monitored, consider adding some expanded clay to the mixture. This acts as a reservoir but keeps the structure open and roots will not suffocate despite the added water content. The clay is marketed under various brand names in the USA and is available in this country.

Roots travel rapidly through this cellular mixture which admits the ideal exchange of air and water and newly repotted trees establish rapidly.

*Repotting/root pruning method*

1. Remove tree from the container. This is a process to be taken gently. Sometimes the tree comes away sweetly but there is usually some binding of the root tips on the container wall. A knife passed vertically round the edge of the root mass helps, but even this may not work. In these extreme cases the best course is to dig a narrow trench round the peripheral area and remove the soil as deeply as possible. Once the soil is away the fingers are passed down the trench and under the root mass. Do not handle or lever the trunk excessively.
2. Root cleansing. Consider the age and species in terms of the roots present and if satisfactory, mark off the outer third of the root mass, using marker sticks if necessary. Wash the outer soil and stroke it away with a pointed stick till the outer third is removed. Repeat the process for the vertical plane.

   Washing shows up the colour differences

**Plate 24** Chinese Juniper aged 25 years. Height 48 cm (1 ft 7 in) spread 61 cm (2 ft $\frac{3}{8}$ in) trunk 5 cm (2 in). Top growth is rank with the form masked, but the roots are in good condition.

**Plate 25** Taken four hours later. Trunk form is re-established. Branches follow the triadic system from outer bend convexities. Covered suspended wires and a light clamp have been used. Rather than lose the abundance of shrubby branches they were stripped for Jin and to preserve and strengthen this element, the trunk has had a ribbon of bark removed. The Shari strip spirals round the trunk and emerges as a Jin.

Plate 26 (*left*) The root mass prior to treatment, vigorous root tips can be seen.

Plate 27 (*above*) The new pot with drainage crocks wired in place.

Plate 28 (*above*) Polythene tie-strings and drainage course in position; strings will be draped out of the way later.

Plate 29 (*right*) The combed root mass prior to evening by shear pruning.

Plate 30 (*below left*) The 'evened' root mass.

Plate 31 (*below right*) The tree placed on the main soil course, seated down and tied. This is a more ambitious sequence than that in *Successful Bonsai Growing*. The Juniper is now growing happily again.

between active pale roots and the ageing, darker material. Prune strong material and the older portions and even the mass. Take half of the exposed beard. If roots are very dense and a little decayed, wash away and prune additional material between heavy surface root areas. Take about 20% of the total at one repot. This will encourage regeneration close to the trunk. Use razor-sharp scissors that cut cleanly. Test them on paper before use and resharpen if doubtful and sterilize with methyl alcohol. Respread the roots and trim back any long ones. Pines can be touchy so take less until familiar with the tree. Clean pot and dry it.

3. Preparing the container and replacing the tree. Place crocking discs over the drainage holes, fine plastic net is ideal, locate with wires, pass strings, either polythene or plastic covered wire up through opposing holes. The strings are passed through the inner sides of the holes, so take-up tension does not shift the discs. Ensure the strings are long enough to knot comfortably then drape out of the way. Pour in 1.25 cm ($\frac{1}{2}$ in) of grit drainage course using heavy particles of 3 mm ($\frac{1}{8}$ in) size. Add soil and check the rootball surface for level; the root mass must be wriggled into the soil to seat it properly so allow for this and the surface of the mass should finish up flush with the container rim.

Bonsai are planted at one-third along the major axis and usually a little behind centre. The decision as to which end is determined by trunk inclination and branch weight. Asymmetrical balance is obtained where the spread of branches is echoed by that of the pot: heavy to the right – plant to the left and so on. If postural changes are needed, the rootball is shaved at the appropriate angle or tilted by raising the soil at one side. Check and recheck, if such changes are made, that the tree is seated firmly. Air pockets can produce root rot. If any work has been done to the roots to alter their shape by wiring or by finger spreading, now is the time to watch carefully as the tie strings are knotted firmly over the mass to locate it.

4. Potting up. Step back from the tree at this point for a final assessment. If happy, add further soil and urge it round the mass with the fingers, employing light pressure. Keep adding soil till the tree starts to feel firm, then level the soil. Moss may be added at this stage using the paste technique. It is better to confine mossed areas to the trunk nucleus till the soil settles. *Never* compress Bonsai soil.

5. Watering. After placing the tree in a lightly shaded spot, give water with a fine sprinkler till it drips from the drainage holes. Keep the tree from direct weather contact for two weeks. Gradually increase the light so the tree is restored to normal location after a further two weeks. The second watering is critical, it should be delayed for a week or more unless dryness dictates otherwise. Foliage sprinkling is beneficial. The situation is essentially as for a cutting.

Do not feed for six weeks or attempt any trunk training in a repotting year. Branches may be lightly treated towards the end of the summer but the danger is in rocking the tree and grinding off new ciliary roots as a result.

# 4 Aesthetics of Bonsai

## AGEING

The aspects listed are simply additions to development techniques, removed from them, but an integral portion of the design.

Fascinating in their use, ageing techniques 'work' through a group of responses they excite in the viewer: visual preconceptions associated with time. Shari is an obvious example of where preconception helps establish the illusion of age in a Bonsai: even where the viewer is the creator of the Bonsai, the visual signals are so strong that while one part of the brain knows the actual age of the plant, another identifies the silver wood and insists the tree is much older.

### *Applications*

TRUNK POSTURE When planted at an angle the seedling will appear older because young saplings are vertical entities – all strength and no taper. Angular changes can also be effected by taper inducement and trunk development techniques. With the exception of the Formal Upright, the more changes in the trunk the better. The actual posture or planting angle is vital in establishing the mood of the tree. Only extensive pictorial study can really explain the nuances as these are so inextricably embodied in the gel of the design – but such study is hardly a discipline!

TRUNK QUALITY Naturally smooth trunk trees must be immaculate and without scar tissue. They are best grown on a programmed basis from cuttings and seeds; Group applications can be stunning and Brooms should have good bark.

Rough bark trees are selected by clone and cultivar and the shortest route is taken to feature texture. In the absence of specimens, cuttings, layerings and grafts are used. The textural aspect is pleasing and the Formal Upright and all the 'mood' styles can be very impressive when trouble is taken with bark texture.

ROOTAGE The pattern of surfaced roots and the articulation with the trunk at the buttress is the important factor. Older trees have eroded systems and saplings have none. Styles which are slanted must have strongly defined anchor roots. Maples may be programmed to feature the tabletop root formation, called after the flared buttress encroaching along the roots, caused by their coalescence. There are illustrations of a Trident Maple featuring this arrangement on pp. 24–25. The picture albums mentioned earlier also give many examples.

SOIL SURFACE The soil of Bonsai can itself take on an aged look when covered with neat and settled mosses of delicate texture. The contours of the soil may be varied and subtly echo the tree. Peat and loam paste is mounded on the surface of the soil and the moss is pressed into this.

BRANCHES Angle is the important element. Young trees have branches Broom-like in their vertical eagerness. The limbs of old trees weep down with just the terminals elevated. Associated with branch development techniques, angular configuration becomes very convincing. The crowns of old trees are rounded or flattened.

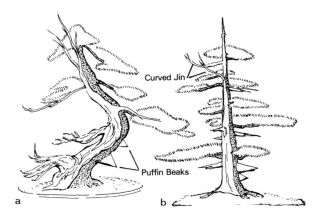

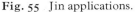

**Fig. 55** Jin applications.
(*a*) Lighter shapes in the Jin look best at the top of the tree or branch terminals. Heavier, curving Jin complement the lower trunk. Note how the 'Puffin Beak' Jin looks out of place on the curving tree.
(*b*) Formal tree. Note how extravagantly curved Jin is out of place on the formal tree.

SCAR TECHNIQUES Where their use is relevant, the techniques of Jin and Sharimiki are both beautiful and convincing, particularly where limbs are pruned to improve the trunk line. Partial or total limb removal, followed by the conversion of the stub by one or both these techniques gives a good result. Trunk shortening as discussed for the Formal Upright style is a legitimate procedure.

The techniques may also be used to add character by echoing the salient Jin or Shari motif through the design. This thematic use must be judged to a nicety otherwise it looks contrived and the tree loses dignity.

## Jin applications

The length and shape of the Jin are first decided. Shaped like puffin's beak; short, fat and pointed Jin give a strong impression (Fig. 55*a*) and are best featured in the lower third of the trunk as are the splayed, fat Jin. Lighter, more linear shapes are best for the upper limbs. Trunk Jin are smoothly pointed and their length should echo trunk taper as far as possible (Fig. 55*b*). All Jin should be sympathetic to the trunk form – a wildly curved Jin on a Formal tree for instance would look ridiculous.

## Jin method

Support the tree and break the branch off at the limit of the Jin. Bark ring the limb at the trunk and then laterally cut through the bark to the heartwood. Peel the bark making sure every trace is removed (Fig. 56*a–d*). Live

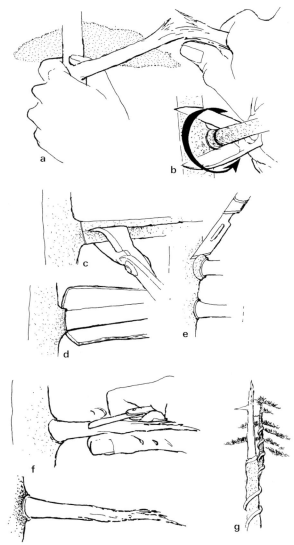

**Fig. 56** Jin method.
(*a*) The limb is broken. (*b*) The bark is roughly scored round with scissors. (*c*) Parallel cuts are made. (*d*) The bark is peeled. (*e*) The bark base is cleaned with a scalpel. (*f*) The Jin is whittled to accord with the tree. (*g*) Trunk Jin: the overlength terminal is stripped and a replacement limb is raised.

material is easily stripped but the bark of dead branches will have to be shaved with a knife. Trim the Jin according to the design (Fig. 56*e*–*f*). Fat Jin may have their ends splayed by twisting with pliers and then ripping the broken segments towards the trunk. Trunk Jin are made in the same way but a new leader is elevated by training a rear branch thus providing a new apex and background to the Jin (Fig. 56*g*).

All incisions through the bark, limiting the peeled area, are made with a scalpel. It is important the bark edge is cleaned so a good callus may form. All freshly peeled wood is allowed a natural drying period of at least two to three months. If desired, Jin may be wired into a fresh form; the new form will be set when the wood has dried. The best period for bark stripping is August, but it must be protected from frost during winter. Paint the dried area in June of the following year with neat lime/sulphur compound. This is an outdoor job – the smell is vile – avoid foliage, soil and skin contact and use an artist's brush with a fine point. This painting preserves the wood, and after repeated applications, silvers it. Jin should be washed and rebleached twice a season for two or three years.

Additional Jin giving the appearance of multi-trunks may be developed by stimulating low shoots. They may be shaped in every way and when bulk and appearance are satisfactory, follow the standard procedures.

## Sharimiki applications

Sharimiki is the removal of live bark from other than terminal portions. The form and extent of the Shari are decided and bark strips adjacent to a Jin for example may be removed, in a manner similar to the natural appearance of old Junipers, showing as white flashes on the trunk. A thin ribbon of bark may be removed – centrally on a Formal tree, spirally, and to one side on an Informal. It is important to take not more than one-third of the available bark diameter.

## Sharimiki method

Limits are set by scalpel incisions and then the

Plate 32  Jin and Sharimiki detail on Needle Juniper.

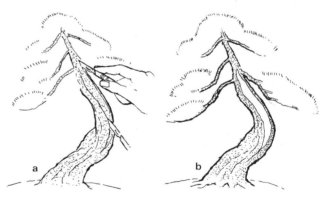

Fig. 57  Sharamiki method.
(*a*) The limbs of the area to be peeled are established with a scalpel. (*b*) The completed Sharamiki.

bark is peeled (Fig. 57). It is advisable to limit the extent of Shari when working with most species and even with Juniper the tree must be in excellent health. To be successful the completed texture of Jin and Shari (unless featuring broken areas) must be smooth and bone-like. The whitened areas sober down and gradually take on the natural silvering of

Fig. 58 Rhythm: explosive and implosive designs.
(*a*) An explosive design is one where the eye is encouraged to find echoes beyond the presence of the tree. The linear form has obvious streamlined properties that generate other responses in the viewer. (*b*) An implosive design is one where the eye is caught up and held inside an economical form and is forced to explore a varied but contained form. The diagram illustrates a typical implosive design where the rhythm constantly returns to the core.

## RHYTHM

In Bonsai the artistic principles of theme and variation are followed as with a well-constructed piece of music or painting, and like these, the Bonsai design must be obedient to its own logic. No matter how subtle, rhythm is implicit in good Bonsai and never more than in the trunk. The trunk may be considered in a number of ways but at all times it remains the armature or core around which the design is formed. To successfully explore theme and variation therefore, a decision as to the preferred end must be taken as soon as possible in the life of the tree, and account taken of possible reshaping, and even the permitted growth rate of the trunk.

Once the basic motif, that is the trunk, has been established, care is taken to explore the variation through the limbs in a repeat sequence. 'Repeat' in this context is defined as recurrent – forms are echoed, not aped.

Rhythm has many aspects, both real and implied. By linear extension a design may appear to explode infinitely outwards (Fig. 58*a*), another may have an implosive quality (Fig. 58*b*), a hieratic grace evocative of sculpture, inside a very limited framework.

Correlations exist between certain types of line and emotional responses. The Hogarth

dead wood. Needless to say, when properly used these techniques are invaluable.

With practice, the major ageing techniques come naturally; when fully exploited their role in stimulating the imagination and refining the design is of inestimable value.

An evolving Bonsai trained to classical standards, that has naturalized ageing elements becomes a superior achievement. The 'ageing' process increases the depth of image in the tree. Young trees tend to shut one out, but confronted with the qualities of age, the mind forms associative images and therefore a sympathy is generated. This fragile quality and the sense of harmony it engenders, is one of the ultimate rewards of Bonsai.

Other elements exist that both heighten the immediate appeal and satisfy objectively (because they have such depth of content), and these are present in all established Bonsai. These are the factors of Rhythm, Texture and Visual Speed.

curve, well known in flower arrangement, is really a relaxed 'S' which is spacious, calm and feminine in feeling (Fig. 59). Angularities generate a stronger but uneasy sensation (Fig. 60). These properties help decide the shapes of the foliage profiles and thereby substantiate design mood and identity at a stroke.

## TEXTURE AND VISUAL SPEED

Time is implicit in the use of the word texture in Bonsai and both tree and container should be touched with its patina. Texture also has great vibrant appeal and this quality, particu-larly with foliage, must be carefully controlled. It is easy to be seduced away from form by an obvious charmer like Chishio Maple. The marrying of rhythm and texture and the degree to which the union is resolved, largely dictates the success of the Bonsai. Linear staccato textures, can be said to have high visual speed, i.e., they sparkle optically. They require careful stabilization by the juxtapo-sition of a visually slow area. A Squamata Meyeri Juniper for instance, in an Informal Cascade arrangement with all the brilliance of blue, gorse-like foliage on a rippled frame of dark brown shaggy bark, would be too rich if not quietened by a deep plain pot. The same

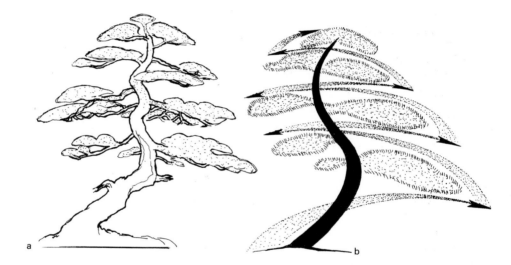

Fig. 59 (*above*)  Rhythm: the Hogarth curve.
(*a*) The success of this design depends on the delicately balanced foliage that emphasizes the feminine grace of the trunk. (*b*) In diagram form, the relationship of core and branch structure becomes clear.

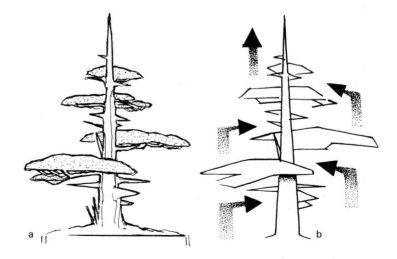

Fig. 60  Rhythm: the angular design.
(*a*) The angular design creates an uneasy, masculine sensation. (*b*) In diagram form the quality of the tree recalls a Samurai in full armour!

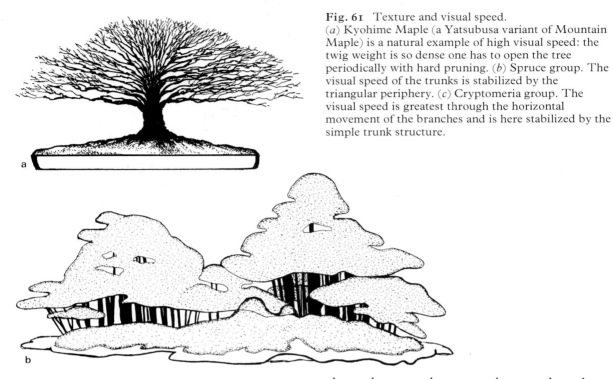

**Fig. 61** Texture and visual speed.
(*a*) Kyohime Maple (a Yatsubusa variant of Mountain Maple) is a natural example of high visual speed: the twig weight is so dense one has to open the tree periodically with hard pruning. (*b*) Spruce group. The visual speed of the trunks is stabilized by the triangular periphery. (*c*) Cryptomeria group. The visual speed is greatest through the horizontal movement of the branches and is here stabilized by the simple trunk structure.

always because these two elements have been smothered. Although discussed separately, the three elements constitute a total aspect and are meaningless apart.

## EVOLUTION IN DESIGN

The following section demonstrates changes in trees over different periods of time and shows another part of the fascination of Bonsai, namely that which lies in the conversion of inspiration into practical techniques. The initial concept is always open to review, for it is important to react freshly to the design; the succeeding section, on Design Assessment, shows the type of thinking necessary at each review.

### Larch group style

Approximately twelve years old from seed. Grown in Surrey. Height 66 cm (2 ft 2 in) spread 94 cm (3 ft 2 in). Unglazed dark brown pot, 62 cm (2 ft 1 in) × 42 cm (1 ft 5 in) × 6 cm (2$\frac{1}{2}$ in). Photographed in summer 1979 (Plate 33) six months after assembly in the Bonsai

qualities are found in a good Group Bonsai where the verticals are slowed down by the broad pan of the earth form (Fig. 61*a*–*c*).

Texture and visual speed therefore contribute 'life' to the design and control the brilliance of linear contrast. They are found in every branch and negative area and where a trained Bonsai appears dull and heavy it is

**Plate 33** Larch group before trimming, summer 1979.

**Plate 34** The same group after training.

pot. Grown for three years in a plastic seed tray. The Group before trimming. Two aspects come over as a result of the hairy appearance: definitions are masked and the trees are leaden; unrestrained branches are shooting up and destroying the aged feeling. The whole structure becomes curiously rigid when the components are out of balance.

*Plate 34.* The Group after training. In this design the idea is to limit the outward visual movement by the firm statements of the peripheral trunks, thus redirecting the eye back into the group and making it explore the subtleties of the trunk rhythms. When the textural outlines of the negative areas were restored, the trunks suddenly came back to life. The right amount of visual speed is now enabling the trunk motif to function clearly but in a manner natural to the species. Understated trunk curves are being picked up in the foliage profiles which are gently domed.

Horizontal and negative areas are working well in the lower regions of the group, but need firmer introduction higher up. This is a natural state of affairs as upper lines are still being related. Thinning will be carried out to simplify the lateral aspects in the way now featured in the peripheral trees and will strengthen the inner trunks. Note the suspended wiring on the first branch of the left tree. Compare with the previous picture. This is the value of line and induction. Just moving one key detail has brought the rhythm back into balance.

The overall contour is triangular, containing three interrelative triangles. As the group matures, the aim is to shift the bias of the chief apex to the right and echo this function through the branches. The effect will be to steepen angles on the right and flatten on the left and this can be seen in embryo in the first branch of the right hand tree. The trunks will then be fully expressed but the change induced will mean a different pot. The present pot is fine for a really formal group but the projected shape will need a softer line and one that will harmonize with the ageing, both real and applied. Natural bark will really show in the next three years. Soil contouring when the

pot is changed will follow the new peripheral bias by mounding under the major tree where at present there is an ugly depression.

## Cryptomeria Formal Upright style

Quoted age thirty-five years. Tree imported from Japan in 1976. Height 71 cm (2 ft 4 in) spread 59 cm (2 ft) trunk 5 cm (2 in). Unglazed dark brown pot, 45 cm (1 ft 6 in) × 35 cm (1 ft 2 in) × 6.25 cm (2½ in).

*Plate 35.* Container grown. The whole tree appears tentative and reflects its true age of about twelve years or so. Basic limb disposition is pleasant but there is a nasty conflict going on between the first and second branches on the left. The hairy growths make assessment difficult but with Cryptomeria, pruning is a constant battle.

*Plate 36.* Same tree transferred to a container with more suitable proportions. Dark grey oval; 54 cm (1 ft 10 in) × 36 cm (1 ft 2 in) × 8 cm (3 in). Photographed in summer 1979. The tree is undergoing grooming. The abrasive second left branch has been shortened and wired to alter position. It has gone from 8 o'clock to 10.30. The trunk has thickened considerably.

*Plate 37.* Grooming complete. Compare with first picture; in 1975 the tree had an implosive shut-in quality, in 1979 the linear force has been reversed by restating negative areas and simplifying trunk/branch junctions. Cleaning underlines has also played its part. Note the difference suspended wire has made to the appearance of the fourth left branch – it is now an important element.

Branch lines are being trained to a triangular profile and plan elevation. The theme is being varied in two ways: the upper profile is in some cases flat, the underline featuring the obtuse apex or the reverse, and, by relating the lengths of branches in the triadic placement, their terminals create further triangles in space, offset from the armature of the trunk – itself conical. The overall periphery is triangular.

Over the past three seasons the tree has been developed by fast growing and feeding but even so, central branch spine weight is

**Plate 35** (*above left*)  Cryptomeria Formal Upright (reproduced from a Japanese nursery 'offering' picture of 1975).

**Plate 36** (*above right*)  Same tree, transferred to more suitable container, summer 1979.

**Plate 37**  Grooming complete, 1979.

poor in the middle tree and the cycle must go on. Coarse growing results as usual in an irregular profile that will only settle down when the tree is correctly finger-pruned. The need for limb weight has delayed the overdue trimming of the first left and right branches and apical area. By lifting at each repotting, the surface roots are improving but have a long way to go before visually supporting the strength of the new structure. At present their structure is about right for the tree's state of development as shown in Plate 35, taken in 1975.

## Chinese Elm Broom style

Twelve years old from a cutting. Raised in Surrey. Height 53 cm (1 ft 9 in) spread 89 cm (3 ft) trunk 7.5 cm (3 in). Unglazed brown oval pot, 53 cm (1 ft 9 in) × 36 cm (2 ft 2 in) × 4.5 cm (1½ in).

*Plate 38*. Taken in summer 1978. The tree has been developed using the growth box technique. The trunk, though showing reasonable taper, is marred at present by the kink above the second left branch. As the tree develops this will become less insistent. One is conscious of the underlying structure but confused by tentative growth points and over-dense foliage, disproportionately placed. Lower branches are flimsy and the root nucleus, though pleasantly radial, is awkwardly emphasized. The pot is absurdly small, neither equalling the diameter of the trunk in depth, nor providing enough visual underpinning of the spread.

*Plate 39*. Taken in summer 1979. The effects of the repotting and transfer to a bigger container, light grey oval 61 cm (2 ft) × 45 cm (1 ft 6 in) × 8.5 cm (3½ in), are obvious in every sense. Spread and height have been kept constant but the trunk already shows a diameter increase of 1.25 cm (½ in). Careful examination shows the effect of the radial root formation on the buttress: the notch in the trunk, bottom right in picture one, has all but vanished and observe the difference in diameter of the lowest branches in direct relation to the new root run. The tree also displays a far more diffused unfolding as a direct result

of the greater root proliferation. Visual speed within the limb mass is being brought into balance, negative areas are more convincing now and there is a significant build-up of tertiary twigs.

As branches of Elms develop they tend to rise, and the lower peripheral potential of Plate 38 is superior to Plate 39, which appears a little too manicured, despite repeated downwards wiring. Almost certainly therefore during 1980, the lower limbs will have to be tied once again, the bark slit to the heartwood and the resulting scar tissue will finally fix the angle with its additional strength. Slits are made at the back. The angular placement is then softened by spreading side branches downwards. The present pot is too deep and the tree too incomplete as a unit to satisfy but there is reasonable potential.

## Trident Maple Informal style

Quoted age about eighty years. Tree imported from Japan in 1970. Height 71 cm (2 ft 4 in) spread 79 cm (2 ft 10 in) trunk 7.5 cm (3 in). Unglazed mid-grey pot, 53 cm (1 ft 9 in) × 38 cm (1 ft 3 in) × 10 cm (4 in).

*Plate 40*. Photographed in spring 1979. The tree has been turned through about 20° to achieve a more asymmetrical form. Although not springing from common whorls, the branches have been so trained that a very evenly distributed tree has resulted. The slight change of viewing angle and the new pot, which stabilizes the general posture, begin to suggest more pleasing height and length differences in the branching.

The foliage was confused at the time of photographing as it was still too early for shoot and side leaf removal techniques, to start neatening the contours. The areas of light glimpsed through the leaf mass will be opened up by selective foliage removal to emphasize branch separations and to create satisfactory negative areas.

*Plate 41*. Taken in summer 1979. Grooming has re-established understructures of each branch and the smaller leaf size helps the profiles appear more natural. Trunk/branch

**Plate 38** Chinese Elm Broom, summer 1978.

**Plate 39** Same tree, transferred to larger container, summer 1979.

**Plate 40** Trident Maple: Informal style, spring 1979.

**Plate 41** Same tree, summer 1979.

junctions have been cleared enough to emphasize the trunk. The trunk rhythm is functioning better, due largely to the contra-relative pull of the first right branch. This draws the eye up the trunk, along the branch and round its periphery in a comma-shaped movement. The branch stabilizes the earth angle and the negative area from periphery to trunk is happy, diverse and easily lost – see Plate 40 – that primary branch fork is vital.

The 'comma' now makes the transposition from directional swing to plastic form: the rounded head of the right branch thinning to the tail of the first left and the motif is then repeated in reverse in the middle tree and reversed again in the head.

There is more sense of lower, middle and upper tree but the middle section is still over strong and tends to give the tree a round-shouldered appearance. This will shortly be countered (a) by branch removal on the right below the head, to open the negative area – there is a branch blocking the rear profile – and (b) by reducing and separating the left middle tree area, which should be twin layered.

## Japanese Yew Semi-Cascade style
Approximately forty years, from a collected tree. Height 30 cm (1 ft), spread from trunk base to lower branch tip 61 cm (2 ft) trunk 5 cm (2 in). Brown pot, 25 cm (10 in) × 25 cm (10 in) × 25 cm (10 in).

*Plate 42*. Photographed in spring 1978. The strongest features of the tree are the hooked trunk base and the root line, the upswinging, left curve of the trunk and the downswept left branch. The tree at this time has just been transplanted into a cascade pot to relate the foliage masses to a deeper container and to prepare it for a more dramatic, descending axis when the root mass permits. The work during 1978 was therefore that of feeding and careful watering to ensure plenty of reserve energy for the hard pruning necessary for additional density of foliage.

*Plate 43*. Photographed in spring 1979. Unglazed brown pot, 22 cm (9 in) × 23 cm (9½ in). In repotting, the tree has been lifted by

another 10 cm (4 in) and the additional trunk movement has added a pleasing thrust line which greatly increases the power of the now steeply raked, lower left branch. To settle the tree at the new angle it is propped on a 'V' shaped wood section on the inner angle, and a heavy plastic restraining string has been taken round the entire unit to prevent the root nucleus surfacing under the leverage.

The foliage has become reasonably dense and the grooming for emphasis of branch and negative areas is taking effect. It is planned to extend the spur of foliage (now directly over the trunk) by another 15 cm (6 in), so the head becomes an umbrella-like form.

When such a large mass is planned, of slow visual speed, it becomes mandatory to enliven it and so additional, domed profiles are planned in the middle and lower branch areas. The existing profiles are simple, reverse form repeats of the head and the negative areas are related 'comma' forms. These will really start to work when the tree is transplanted into a narrower, taller pot and the floating quality will be greatly enhanced.

## Trident Maple Root Over Stone style
Quoted age forty years. Tree imported in 1977. Height 45 cm (1½ ft) spread 38.5 cm (1 ft 3 in) trunk 5 cm (2 in). Unglazed dark brown pot, 29 cm (1 ft) × 20 cm (8 in) × 7.5 cm (3 in).

*Plate 44*. As a unit there is an integrated quality and the planting has done well for a ten-year-old, field grown tree, or rather trees (there are two). The rock may be classified as tall and the planting as belonging to the 'old trunk' category. The curve of the stone takes the eye clockwise, first round the stone terminating below the round, knob-like projection and then round again, over the foliage which repeats the form of the stone. The repeat is not literal but sufficiently akin to satisfy.

*Plate 45*. Taken in summer 1977. Mid brown pot, 53 cm (1 ft 9 in) × 41 cm (1 ft 4 in) × 7.5 cm (3 in). The tree was damaged in transit and lost its terminal shoot – newly created in Japan by the spur replacement

**Plate 42**  Japanese Yew: Semi-cascade style, spring 1978.

**Plate 43** (*right*)  Same tree, re-potted, spring 1979.

**Plate 44**  Trident Maple: Root over Stone style (reproduced from a Japanese nursery 'offering' picture of 1976).

**Plate 45** (*above*)  Same tree (as Plate 44), summer 1977. New leader and branch extensions have been formed.

**Plate 46** (*right*)  Same tree, summer 1979. Major postural change effected by turning the face of the stone to 5 o'clock.

technique – and most of the branches which were also recently spur developed.

The new leader and branch extensions have been formed in the UK by the techniques discussed in the section on Branch Formation

The leader and bowed right branch are already wire set. The leader has been stopped twice – compare its taper with the right branch which has grown unchecked. Damage such as this is doubly infuriating in that one is forced to compromise for the sake of even development, and so one falls between the twin poles of maintenance and extension and of the balance between.

The secondary tree on the right now appears distinct. The two trunks have in fact grafted themselves together (or have been helped) and the union is spoilt by the nasty bump near the main trunk. The bump is the base of a useful down-curved, back branch, possibly a useful source of foliage to mask the bump. The peripheral motif found in the stone is still there but is being extended to make better sense of the design.

*Plate 46*. Taken in summer 1979. Light brown pot, 61 cm (2 ft) × 43 cm (1 ft 5 in) × 6 cm (2 in). The tree was rewired before repotting in spring 1979. A major postural change has been effected by turning the face of the stone to 5 o'clock. The eye now follows the same line but moves up the root formation in a natural way. The thrust and rhythm have been greatly enhanced and now the trunk really flows from root to apex in a slow 'S'. The 'S' motif is repeated in a gentle, upward spiral from dome to adjacent under-branch across the structure. The periphery still remains an echo of the stone. Contours are being established by shoot and side leaf pruning accompanied by sub-branch wiring.

The ground pattern is dull and in need of domed contours. The whole planting should be raised, so the rock appears on an eminence. Now the elements of the design are once more in balance, the tree can be coarse grown during 1980 to thicken up the diameters of the new portions and will be hacked back hard during July, refined for a month, and the cycle repeated yearly until the spur diameters begin

to match the 1977 stubs. It will take another five years or so before the trunk and branches lose their newly made appearance.

## Chinese Juniper Driftwood style

Quoted age one hundred years. Tree imported from Japan in 1971. Height 61 cm (2 ft) spread 61 cm (2 ft) trunk 6.25 cm (2½ in). Unglazed brown pot, 40 cm (1 ft 4 in) × 28 cm (11 in) × 10 cm (4 in).

*Plate 47*. A newly styled mountain tree. Trunk diameter was a bonus: it in fact measured 10 cm (4 in) from a different angle. One's immediate reaction was to layer or Jin, the hook shaped top section, but instead, after careful inspection the reverse elevation was chosen as the display angle and the top was retained.

The new 'front' presented better depth potential through the design and the feeling was that perhaps the wrong side of the tree had been photographed. The weakest aspect of the new front was the very one-sided root development. This and the obviously concave trunk section (see Plate 48) and its abrupt, but naturally formed, diameter difference at the first branch, must mean the tree was developed by the trunk splitting technique described by Ian Price in the section on Sharimiki (p. 40).

The tree had been very badly treated prior to shipment: the profiles had been clipped for photographic cosmetic purposes and as a result, the appearance for the next five years was marred and refinement impeded by persistent, gorse-like Oxycedrus growth. This juvenile growth is difficult to treat when an old tree like this is in poor condition. Eventually sound feeding and light pruning won it round.

*Plate 48*. The new front, summer 1979. Height 81 cm (1 ft 8 in) spread 81 cm (1 ft 8 in) trunk diameter remains constant at 10 cm (4 in). Unglazed mixed grey pot, 53 cm (1 ft 9 in) × 37 cm (1 ft 3 in) × 14 cm (6 in). The form is now based on the major trunk movements and the curves of those two sections. Looked at quickly, the sensation is of a head and two branches that balance the double curve. That is the primary triangle. Looked at

**Plate 47** Chinese Juniper: Driftwood style (reproduced from a Japanese nursery offering picture of 1970).

**Plate 48** New front of same tree, summer 1979.

again, the head breaks into three, making five elements and when complete, each of the five will be sub-divided into threes. The foliage motif is a simple, tripartite dome with a convex base.

The eye swings from the root to the first right branch, around it, across the line of the first left branch, follows that, and so on to the top. There is a feeling of repose in the tree largely stemming from the triangular form and the seesawing action on the eye that just brings it back into balance.

Though visual speed is often rapid through the incidental linear rhythm of the Jin, the slow-moving texture of the foliage size and shape restore balance and this type of texture and contour are found again in the pot.

The underside of the first left branch will be pruned to emphasize the concave form. This simply means removing the weaker foliage; the crescent shape will sit more happily on the right-angled branch. The central right branch will be trimmed back to the curved line of shadow occurring at one third of its length.

The effect of these two reductions will be to swing the bias from the lower left crescent over to the first right branch, and in the case of the second reduction, to push the line of the head further left. The combined result will make the tree far more asymmetric and balance will depend on a pendulum controlled by evolving foliage mass and detail.

## Scots Pine Informal style

Estimated age sixty years, from a collected tree. Height 30 cm (1 ft) spread 55 cm (1 ft 10 in) trunk 3.5 cm (1 in). Unglazed red pot, 30 cm (1 ft) × 20 cm (8 in) × 7.5 cm (3 in).

Prior history. The tree was collected from a wet site in August 1962. Existing branches were tapered but very long. The roots were surprisingly compact, due to the presence of heather peat around the trunk. Main branches were reduced by cutting terminals back and the tree was then planted in a large box. Soil was very light and consisted mainly of sand, leaf mould and pine needle. The box was plunged in a side flower border without protection. At this time needle growth was in meagre, yellow tufts and confined to the terminal areas. Then followed the record breaking 1962/63 winter, but amazingly, the tree survived.

By 1963 – year 1 – the tree resembled a flat 'T' and it was still too early to tackle style, so instead longer shoots were lightly finger pinched to trigger inner branch activity. Combined with feeding during the summer, copious budding was produced at *primary*, and secondary shoot bases, significant because an ageing Pine is reluctant to produce buds this far back. More feeding and August-reduction pruning, to all but three pairs of leaves on terminals, produced an explosion of shoots during 1964 – year 2 – and 1965 – year 3. The second year followed the same pattern but some wire training was carried out and some bolder reduction pruning. Wiring was of the simplest type – suspended guy wires from nailed areas in the box wall, but this method proved positive enough to curve the totally straight branches.

*Plate 49.* 1966 – year 4. The tree was repotted for the first time in spring 1965 using light soil composed chiefly of pea gravel, leaf mould and pine needle. The primitive methods produced a tree whose periphery depends on topiary techniques but as such, is triadically sound. Up to this time, information on treating Scots Pine was impossible to obtain, and it was really 'fingers crossed' and hope for the best, recording and analysing everything.

*Plate 50.* 1977 – year 15. Height 36 cm (14 in) spread 77 cm (2 ft 7 in) trunk 6.25 cm (2½ in). Unglazed brown pot, 40 cm (1 ft 4 in) × 28 cm (11 in) × 7.5 cm (3 in). Over a period of eleven years the juvenile planes have vanished and the triadic placement has settled. The most important styling change was the lowering of the right hand, head fork, seen in Plate 49. This was accomplished with the aid of a mild steel plate former. The former was shaped in a single arc and tied along the branch, cushioning the friction areas and the terminal was lowered, by suspension, taking the branch with it. The branch was lowered by 5 cm (2 in) per year. This of course was very gradual but there were no reference

**Plate 49** (*above*)  Scots Pine:
Informal style (reproduced from
a photograph taken in 1966).

**Plate 50** (*right*)  Same tree,
1977.

**Plate 51** (*below*) Same tree,
1979.

Plate 52 Satsuki
Azalea: Twin
trunk style,
summer 1979.

points and in any case the tree was old. As this branch became separated, it was wired to the shallow dome profile and this theme was followed over the whole plant. The most effective means of making the tree more dense was the annual August trimback. Through this it was possible by bud stimulation to reduce the branches from their initial, sparsely foliaged, 90 cm (3 ft) span, to 45 cm (1½ ft), and rebuild gradually. August pruning is gentle and the gnarled branch terminals are an almost incidental bonus.

*Plate 51.* 1979 – year 17. Dimensions remain constant. The container is now an unglazed grey pot, 47 cm (1 ft 7 in) × 37 cm (1 ft 3 in) × 13 cm (5 in). Through 1978 and 1979 the emerging shoots were the subject of deep pinching and this has produced dense budding. Left and right branches have been lowered and the design is coming into full power. A great part of the visual satisfaction in the unit lies in the narrowed and better expressed negative areas. These are really enlivening the design and will be increased where the head is impinging on the left branch and through the needle mass. A start has already been made to introduce these features by opening and regrouping the isolated sub-profiles, shown by the areas of darker

shadows. The increased element of visual speed will make a great difference.

## DESIGN ASSESSMENT
### Satsuki Azalea Twin Trunk style
Quoted age forty years when imported in 1970. Height 49 cm (1 ft 8 in) spread 77 cm (2 ft 7 in) trunk base 13 cm (5 in) left trunk 7.5 cm (3 in) right trunk 5 cm (2 in). Unglazed brown pot, 45 cm (1½ ft) × 30 cm (1 ft) × 10 cm (4 in). Photographed in summer 1979.

*Plate 52.* 1979. The tree is marred by the relative discrepancy in the diameter of the trunks – the minor is the fat one. Correction is being attempted through development of the major trunk. The basic posture is acceptable, the trunks blend well and have character, the bole is strong, convincingly flared and successfully initiates trunk/branch rhythm. Finer detail and profiles are a bit masked at present due to the growing-on technique but are still sufficiently visible to show the allied branch structure.

When imported, the tree had just been lifted from a growing bed and existing 'branches' were one-year shoots, of matchstick diameter, coiled with wire three times their thickness. By 1977, the tree was well branched

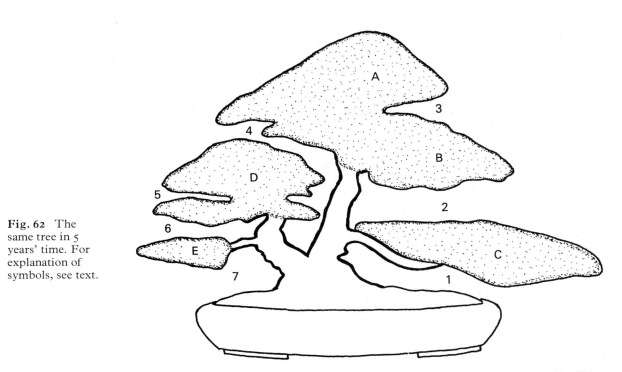

**Fig. 62** The same tree in 5 years' time. For explanation of symbols, see text.

and imposingly contoured but serious, detailed work on it had not yet been undertaken. After flowering in 1977, the tree was stripped way back to secondary structures and rewired. This was repeated in 1978 and the basic profiles, though hairy and universally in need of lateral wiring, were at least arranged honestly, if not 'effectively'. Apart from its obvious root development capacity, the pot does absolutely nothing for the design which needs a softer line more in keeping with foliage profiles and branch angles.

*Fig. 62.* 1985. The tree in five years' time. The minor trunk form is a reversed repeat of the major which shows height and diameter increase. Immediate impressions are of three elements: minor, major and branch 'C', but closer inspection shows there are really five elements, each of which has an echoed counterpart.

'C' carries the eye powerfully away from the trunk but the change of plane in the understructure checks the flow visually, stabilizing the whole rhythm. This contra-relative check is a useful device. The branch is flatter, and features the softened diamond elevation. Negative area 1 is narrower and longer and reinforces the power of 'C'.

'E' is the exact counterpart of 'C'. The length shows little increase but the branch has been refined and flattened. Negative area 7 is broader than 1 and this clearly relates the left hand edge of the bole to the container and is an interesting contrast to 1, which has a shadowy, masked quality. 'A/B' and 'D' follow the same pattern. Negative areas 2 and 6 are interestingly akin to each other. Areas 3 and 5 are just echoes but negative area 4 is a key element as the 'thick and thin' aspect directly affects the potency of everything else.

The new container is a grey oval measuring 53 cm (1 ft 9 in) × 36 cm (1 ft 2 in) × 9 cm (4 in) chosen for the simple line and curved section that usefully states the main theme and terminates it by reversal.

### Chinese Juniper Cascade style
Estimated age forty years. From an old collection acquired in May 1979. Head to lowest point 82 cm (1 ft 9 in) spread 64 cm (2 ft 2 in) trunk 3 cm (1 in). Unglazed grey pot, 30 cm (1 ft) square, 18 cm (7 in) deep. The tree shown in the repotting sequence was from the same collection, and in the 'before' shot, parallels the previous condition of this tree. Photographed in late June 1979.

**Plate 53** Chinese Juniper: Cascade style, summer 1979.

*Plate 53.* The tree was so completely over-developed, it was one straight mat but the roots were in good order, so it was decided to restyle and repot the tree in the same season rather than let it waste further energy. The restyling exercise was rather like reclaiming a topiary cockerel! Vestiges were there but the branches had straightened and exhibited the strong, plumose form of the species. The trunk alone preserved its form, although even to find this one had to burrow through and divide the foliage in bunches.

The picture shows the basic arrangement with major branches restated and redundancies stripped for Jin. Wire used is plastic-clad to soften the friction points. In view of the need to repot, detailed work on minor branching was delayed because of its irritating effect on the plant and this has created the visual fuzziness and lack of resolution. The tree was repotted after styling and the roots were given the standard treatment. Afterwards the unit was propped with a wooden 'T' piece to prevent the trunk resting on the pot and the surface nucleus was secured with plastic-clad wires passed up through the drainage holes and secured over the bole area. Additional wires were passed round the outside of the pot and tied. The tree felt reasonably firm and was placed immediately in a well lit and ventilated

greenhouse and watered in using Vitamin $B_1$ solution for the soil and straight water for the foliage. Foliage was misted daily like a cutting and the colour went from yellow to blue-green in a month. Feeding schedules produced enough tip growth to warrant pinching by August.

*Fig. 63.* The tree after five years. The trunk apex supporting branches 'A, a and B' is much thickened and reflects the additional weight of these profiles. A curving rhythm has been established based on the five elements that flow from 'A a–E e' allowing the eye visual passage through the foliage, equalling the speed of the trunk and strengthened with the coexistent zigzag formed by the understructure: 'A–a; a–C; C–d; d–e'. Negative areas 1, 2 and 3 set the theme and appear easily controlled, but in fact their contours are as cogent as the interior foliage forms. The foliage contours depend on a triadic bubble motif which the negative areas must repeat. The long, thin end of area 3 is particularly critical as this visually supports major axial movement. The inner gaps between 'D–d, E–e' and areas 4, 5 and 6 need careful maintenance as their shape controls the bias shift of each form. Area 7 is the gauge by which trunk angle is judged.

The creation of the branch foliage profile is

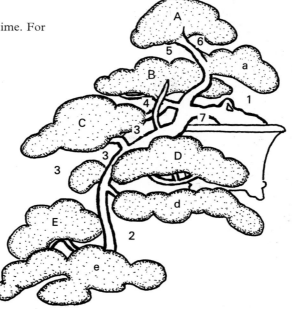

**Fig. 63** The same tree in 5 years' time. For explanation of symbols, see text.

a matter of shoot extension and the *slow* process of wiring laterals and arranging their tips in contiguous terminal bubbles. The terminals, then the secondary shoots are pinched, and so on, the growth spreading sideways and newly arranged bubbles linking up, presenting a smooth profile. If a sense of the bubble formation is preserved the tree is more interesting.

## Cork Bark Pine Informal style

Quoted age seventy-five years when imported in 1972. Height 77 cm (2 ft 7 in) spread 77 cm (2 ft 7 in) trunk 10 cm (4 in). Unglazed dark red pot, 55 cm (1 ft 10 in) × 42 cm (1 ft 5 in) × 16 cm (6 in).

*Plate 54.* Photographed in summer 1979. Prior history: apart from the trunk, the tree was untrained except for pompon foliage masses. Needle colour was yellow but this was caused by Californian sun scorch. The exporter claimed that the tree, then planted in a 45 cm (1½ ft) pot, 30 cm (1 ft) deep, would not need repotting for twenty years. Despite being freighted by sea fully-potted, it soon became obvious there was soil trouble. The tree was given a modified soil mixture and a shallower pot and this seemed temporarily to clear the problem but it became necessary to use a large box during 1973 and this definitely helped – the foliage colour deepened.

Once back in a Bonsai container in 1975, the foliage went from yellow to green and back every other month. It was obvious that faulty drainage and soil were not the cause, so, with a full complement of aids to hand, a major root overhaul took place in spring 1977. All major branches were cut back hard, reducing them by at least 50%. A peripheral trench was dug and the tree lifted out carefully avoiding bark contact. Roots were teased out by brushing the soil outwards from the mass. The answer became clear when a tap root old enough to have mature bark and approximately 4 cm (1½ in) thick and 45 cm (1½ ft) long was revealed. The root roughly followed the rectangle and its inner portion was packed with grey Japanese clay. Roots pendant from the tap root terminal contributed ¾ of the available root fibre; the other ¼ were mercifully distributed among surface radials. The pot was prepared in the usual way but with copious tie strings, a very deep drainage course, and a soil mix of three parts pine needle, two parts leaf mould, one of peat and two of grit.

The tap root was shortened by 30 cm (1 ft) and the clay nodule was removed. Every care was taken to preserve other available ciliary

**Plate 54** Cork Bark Pine: Informal style, summer 1979.

roots in potting and tie strings were secured to cross every point of the root nucleus. The roots were watered in with vitamin $B_1$ solution, foliage was water misted and bottom heat supplied by placing the pot over soil-heating cables. Foliage was misted twice daily and bottom heat was discontinued after a month when bud activity began.

After fifteen months of continual protection the tree grew appreciably and in spring 1979 it was virtually potted on into the present container, root disturbance being confined to combing out peripheral areas to make an outward facing beard. Soil mix was identical to that used in the first re-potting.

The tree had now grown enough for styling to be safe and worthwhile, and to date displays five foliage elements of a triangular form, two of which are located in the upper tree and three in the middle and lower.

*Fig. 64.* The tree after five years. The chief differences are in the extra lengths of 'C' and 'E' and in the reduction of the bulk of 'A'. Detailed work is neatening profiles and their character appears precise instead of accidental.

The two triangles formed previously now interrelate convincingly, like opposing kite forms. The acute angle formed by the terminals of 'D'/'E' is echoed by the terminals of 'A'/'a' and the obtuse angles of each are formed by the upper profiles of 'A'/'B' and 'D'/'C' respectively.

The overall periphery is triangular but there is a curved rhythm formed by the terminals from 'A'–'E' that straightens at the apex of 'A' and drops down to 'a' and recurs in the domed profiles of 'C' and 'E'. These, and the understructures of 'C' and 'E' with their opposing, contra-relative checking of angular flow, are in fact all based on the forms found in the trunk.

In a design with a Pine like this, where needle growth is long and visual speed high, negative areas are of equal importance and are maintained by August grooming and winter wiring. Feeding is the key to adventitious budding, and reduction pruning, the only safe way to reduce needle length and encourage density. The most touchy negative areas are 3 and 4, which if overgrown, immediately deaden the image and render the tree top-heavy as in Plate 54. Area 5 is also tricky, coming at the axial change – it should be cleared away enough to clarify but not to make stark.

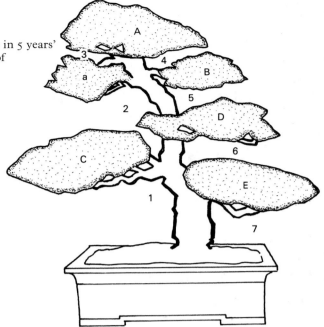

**Fig. 64** The same tree in 5 years' time. For explanation of symbols, see text.

## Scots Pine Informal style

Approximately forty years old, from a collected tree. Height 41 cm (1 ft 4 in) spread 71 cm (2 ft 5 in) trunk 9 cm (4 in). Unglazed grey pot, 41 cm (1 ft 4 in) × 30 cm (1 ft) × 14 cm (6 in).

*Plate 55*. Taken in summer 1979. Prior history: collected in June 1973 (year 1), the tree was growing in the top of an old wall scheduled for demolition. The tree was collected forty-eight hours ahead of the bulldozers. As it had been admired for the previous 11 years, the advance warning was doubly fortunate.

A full collecting kit was taken, as the Pine was growing between the top and second courses and a little site clearance was envisaged. Once on the ladder however, removal could not have been easier, the bricks and mortar were rotten and one or two light blows separated the courses, exposing the root, beautifully developed and fibrous – one brick wide and three metres long. The Pine was simply lifted off the wall, taken down the ladder, root-wrapped and transported home.

The initial stage was not photographed which is particularly unfortunate as the branches proved as long as the roots. Another aspect of the root/branch correlation which was interesting was their allied nature: both were narrow and linear; there was virtually no depth at all through the branches, making the tree appear like a vertical, cardboard cutout and the roots were equally flat horizontally, having grown along the mortar course.

Branches were straight and superbly tapered with 90% of available foliage confined to terminal areas. The needles were minute, meagre and yellow and the buds thin and poorly marked, the whole impression being of a skeletal fan.

The tree was placed at eye level and wherever possible, terminals pruned back to activate side branches and even the terminals of these were removed in the bid to promote inner branch activity. This seemed hopeful because the roots were extraordinarily well furnished with ciliaries. Root length reduction was therefore equally straight-forward, the idea being, as usual, to maintain balance. Eventually the three-metre spread was reduced to two metres and the tree was planted diagonally in a temporary container with most of the roots arranged straight out from the trunk, and just the outer third bent round the walls. It was felt the outer root bending would not matter because this would be sacrificed at the next repotting and meanwhile, suppres-

**Plate 55**   Scots Pine: Informal style, summer 1979.

sion of terminal root activity would help force the formation of inner buds.

Soil used consisted of 60% pine needle and 40% coarse grit. No pressure was used, the soil was sifted around the roots and carried in with the fingers. The unit was placed in a lightly shaded, cool greenhouse, watered in well, and left strictly undisturbed. The needles were misted daily. By August, existing lateral buds had plumped up by about 200% and were bright red. There were some adventitious bud breaks on current and previous year's wood, current year needle growth not yet 'set' on collection had lengthened, and colour was deepening.

1974 – year 2. During 1974 the Pine was well fed and new terminals were soft pinched in May, taking 50%, to allow some new needle development but also to strengthen the first generation adventitious buds. No other styling was attempted. During August, secondary budding from the terminals was matched by activity among the first generation inner buds. Terminals were therefore shortened a little more.

1975 – year 3. Shoot and terminal pruning were maintained in May and August and main branches were lowered using cushioned, suspension guys taken to nailed wall points. This change immediately softened the tree and by late summer, side branches were selected for terminal replacement. Branch reduction was determined by the strength and growth of the 1973, first generation adventitious buds, and the presence of needle growth to help nurture the production of further buds. The tree width was reduced by another 90 cm (3 ft) and terminals re-established with wiring.

Two seasons of pruning had produced clumps of needles and these were thinned and side limbs wired, to conform with the suspended limbs. The lightening, always from the periphery inwards, countered the coarse growth necessary for development, but offensive in appearance. By this time, the first generation inner buds were ascertainable entities and were lightly wired to help form the foliage domes.

1976 – year 4. In March the tree was repotted and planted in a deep, broad Bonsai

STYLING COLLECTED TREES: SCOTS PINE
**Colour Plate 65.** Top: October 1986. The tree has been solidly established for three seasons.

**Colour Plate 66.** Above: Basic trunk/branch junctions cleaned of foliage. Bottom left branch curved forward with steel bar and block.

**Colour Plate 67.** Top: Bottom left branch styled with wire and scissor thinning.

**Colour Plate 68.** Above: Bottom right branch styled.

**Colour Plate 69.** Top: Middle tree styled.               **Colour Plate 70.** Above: The basic styling complete.

**Colour Plate 71.**
Above: Branch curving
detail of steel bar and
block.
**Colour Plate 72.**
Top right: November
1986. The tree after
some fine adjustment
has a more refined
outline.
**Colour Plate 73.**
Right: Spring 1987.
Repotted into a large
oval, the tree appears
underpotted still!
The answer is to bring
the lines of the lower
branches in a little to
shorten the spread.
This will make the
tree/pot combination
more successful.

STYLING COLLECTED TREES: COMMON
JUNIPER
**Colour Plate 74.** Top left: Tree established in
temporary, overlarge container.
**Colour Plate 75.** Top right: Change of angle shows
better trunk line.
**Colour Plate 76.** Bottom left: Trunk cleaning and
some bark stripping begins.
**Colour Plate 77.** Bottom right: The bark. The
stripped area follows a natural, silvered wound area.

**Colour Plate 78.** Top left: The tree thinned and wired.
**Colour Plate 79.** Top right: A slight overhead view enhances the branch depth. This indicates that the tree will be tilted forward when repotted.
**Colour Plate 80.** Above: The back.

STYLING COLLECTED TREES: COMMON JUNIPER

**Colour Plate 81.** Opposite: Tree established for two seasons in a temporary, deep container. Winter 1985/86.
**Colour Plate 82.** Centre right: After a season's growth the tree is ready for styling. October 1986.
**Colour Plate 83.** Right: Trunk cleaned and lower limbs stripped.

**Colour Plate 84.** Right: Trunk detail showing cleaned bark and silvered areas.
**Colour Plate 85.** Below: Twin apex jinned and fluted with electric router.
**Colour Plate 86.** Below right: Pot tilted to indicate future growing angle.
**Colour Plate 87.** Bottom: Wiring and trimming complete.

For the most recent photograph, Spring 1987 repotted into lighter container more in keeping with the flow of the trunk, see colour plate 34.

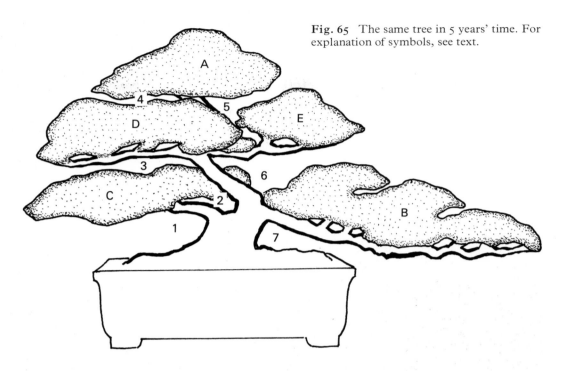

**Fig. 65** The same tree in 5 years' time. For explanation of symbols, see text.

pot and the heavy surface root at left was pruned back to even the vigour of the mass that remained remarkably fibrous. The root mass was a solid block of mycelium, the beneficial white mould that grows in association with healthy Pine roots. Soil used was pine needle, peat and grit in equal parts.

1979 – year 7. Transplanted into present pot in 1978. Over the last two seasons the branches have finally been cut deep enough to promote branching close in to the trunk and these new terminals are being extended. The profiles now consist of 'inner bud' growths only – all older terminal areas have gone.

Posture is re-established: the upper trunk is a little rigid but makes for strength and echoes the straightness of the lower right side of the trunk. The initial image is of an upturned 'L' and a triadic arrangement, that also forms a triangle between terminals. Further triangles occur through foliage profiles, understructures and negative areas. It is still too soon for the design to have resolution and clamps are still necessary to combat the straightness of the original main branches.

*Fig. 65* – the tree in five years' time. The

relationship remains unchanged but additional foliage weight and the extension of 'B', 'C' and 'D' have slowed the angular speed making a more integrated unit. The 1979 image has a visually frantic quality, stemming from the zigzag between negative areas 1 through 'B', back to 'C', 'E' and so on which gathers momentum over every straight passage unimpeded by profiled, parabolic curves. The almost equal black and white values of foliage and negative area aggravate the issue.

Negative areas now read as sublimated zones and this allows the eye time to study detail without the previous flicker effect. The domed heads slow the rhythm as it dips over the crown of each, instead of exploding outwards along each angled plane.

This softening of angle is repeated in negative areas 1–7 and gives new depth to the design by varying 'young' straight lines and contributing incidental interest. The bones of the tree are enhanced, not muffled, but the new rhythms must be carefully balanced by maintenance of profiles.

Through the curving in areas 1 and 2, the

Plate 56  Scots Pine: Informal
Upright style, summer 1979.

eye now swings into 'C' and accepts the logic –
it could be another tree – it feels right. The
shapes 3, 4 and 5, are obviously critical in
lightening 'A', 'D', 'E', and 6 and 7 repeat
each other in reverse, thus taking off the
natural harshness of the trunk at those points.
'B' locks the design and its triple slowing
action and contra-relative thrust are reversed
in 'C' and repeated through the domes of 'A',
'D' and 'E'. The pot is now in doubt and a
lipped oval of a more curved section would be
better.

## Scots Pine Informal Upright style
Approximately thirty years old, from a collected tree. Height 71 cm (2 ft 4 in) spread
77 cm (2 ft 7 in) trunk 6.5 cm (3 in). Unglazed
brown pot, 56 cm (1 ft 10 in) × 36 cm (1 ft
2 in) × 9 cm (4 in).
   *Plate 56.* Photographed in summer 1979.
Prior history: collected in 1972 (year 1). Roots
were excellently developed and very compact,
the tree having come from a wet peat area that

dried in the summer. The tree terminated at
the junction of the first left branch and
vestiges of the terminal whorl removed at the
time are just visible.
   1973 – year 2. By spring 1973 budding was
so good and the root system so strong that the
Pine was bedded out for development. The
site chosen was sloping and well-drained, so
extra peat and sandy soil mixture were worked
into the ground as added root conditioners in
case drainage proved too sharp.
   The first left branch, actually composed of
two whorled limbs, was loosely positioned
with wire and a new leader was elevated – at
this time not long enough to reach the first
right branch! The roots were spread radially
over the worked area and then extra mix plus
garden soil was added and the root system was
firmed lightly.
   1975 – year 4. During 1973 and the next
seasons the leader was allowed free extension
but checked and wired each August. First and
second points are discernible as angular chan-

**Fig. 66** The same tree in 5 years' time. For explanation of symbols, see text.

ges in the trunk. A new leading shoot and one lateral were retained at each pruning, thus forming the first right, rear and second left branches. The third trunk pruning was carried out high enough to allow the head to develop through a weeping branch arrangement that would not interfere with the lower branches. No feeding was carried out.

1976 – year 5. The Pine was transferred to a growth box in spring 1976 using a soil mix of pine needle, peat and grit. The roots were somewhat unkempt but vigorous. After establishment the tree was fed monthly and shoots were pinched lightly in May and shortened in August. The tree felt firmly rooted in August, so during the 1976/77 winter period, main branches were given their directions with wire and lowered, using guy wires to nailed wall points.

1977 – year 6. Feeding and the May/August soft and hard pruning schedules produced the familiar needle pompons and these were lightened by reducing the number of shoots at common points, and wiring laterals to conform to branch lines. Copious budding of

the inner areas made terminal reduction possible. It was decided to repot and really surface and distribute the roots.

1978 – year 7. The repotting was carried out in spring using the present container and the standard mix. Endless trouble was taken to lift and feature the true base of the trunk and the roots were teased out and realigned to enhance the bole. Covered wire staple forms were used to peg the roots and make them conform to the new soil contour. As a result of the general root disturbance and 1977 terminal reduction, the whole plant 'made haste slowly' and it was not till August, when the first feeds were given, that buds really plumped and needles completed their current year development. A year of quiet activity is a good thing.

1979 – year 8. The tree grew happily in 1979 and very evenly, making it possible to restructure branches with further lateral wiring and suspension and achieve a basic unity. The design now reads triadically as first left branch, middle tree and head, with the middle tree firmly within the triangle of apex and the base formed by left and right low branch terminals. If looked at quickly it appears as 3, then 5, 7 and ultimately 9. All the elements should be seen clearly and allowance made for evolution, a prematurely complete tree is a very over-wrought thing and one must tolerate roughness and approximation of a plant in training. Once this is understood, the aggravation caused by incompleteness vanishes.

*Fig. 66*. After a further five years of necessary roughness the elements are coming into balance. The basic relationship is unchanged but the content is deepened through the less casual rhythm that now spirals round the tree from 'A' to 'B'.

The tree 'works' because the acute angle of the terminals 'B'/'C'/'E' supplies the appropriate 'snub nose' in relation to the trunk convolutions and in contrast to the individual, acutely angled terminals at 'D', 'G'; and 'A'. The balance of brevity and extension is really an exploitation of the primary bole notch in relation to the wider trunk movement and the motif is repeated through the tree.

**Plate 57**   Scots Pine:
Literati/Triple Trunk style, 1978.

**Plate 58**   Same tree, summer 1979.

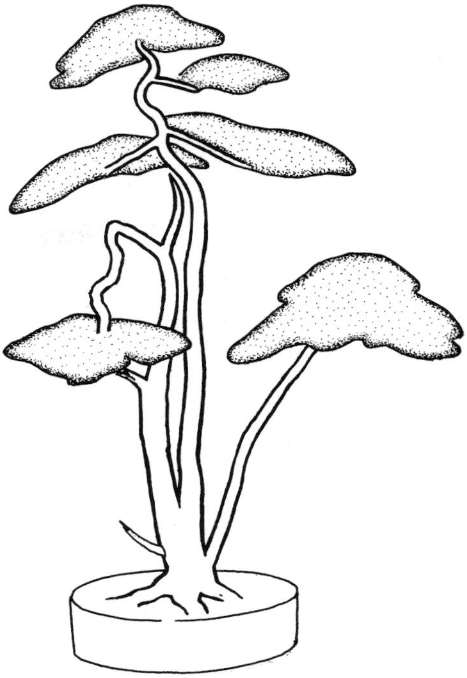

Plate 59    Same tree, spring 1980.

Fig. 67    The same tree in 1982. The tree now
has the soft rhythm of the Literati.

## Scots Pine Literati/Triple Trunk style

Classifiable as either style. Approximately fifty years old, from a collected tree. Height 86 cm (2 ft 10 in) spread 66 cm (2 ft 2 in) trunks 10 cm (4 in). Unglazed brown pot, 30 cm (1 ft) × 10 cm (1 ft).

*Plate 57.* Photographed in 1978. Prior history: 1976 – year 1. The tree was collected from a wet peat site in August 1975 and established in the standard manner. Roots, and therefore buds, were good and light shoot pruning was possible in July 1976. The tree was fed in August and a very heavy branch was pruned and stripped on the major trunk. During the winter 1976/77 period basic branch wiring reinforced the related character of the trunks but showed up a nasty linear clash between the trunk lines at the heads of primary and secondary limbs.

1977 – year 2. Feeding, May and August pruning and further wiring initiated the inner bud detail and fuller profiles, but aggravated the apical clash.

1978 – year 3. The tree as it appeared in August 1978. Everything has been attempted to separate and clarify the trunk lines. The clamp on the tertiary trunk is to try to form an echo of the natural bends in the other trunks of the tree.

*Plate 58.* 1979 – year 4. Photographed in summer 1979. The primary trunk has been shortened and the tip stripped and shaped for Jin and the mid branch further treated. Already there is an improvement, the secondary trunk now becomes the primary and will gradually overtake the former in diameter as foliage weight increases.

*Plate 59.* 1980 – year 5. Photographed outside in spring 1980. New red pot, 33 cm (1 ft 1 in) × 12 cm (5 in). Side view. This shows the perspective through the grouping; the trunk bases and the newly surfaced radial roots. The tree has been completely restyled by wiring.

*Fig. 67* – the tree in two years. The shapes established in 1980 have now been resolved and the tree has the agreeable, soft rhythm of the Literati. The pot is a little heavy and might be changed for a lighter design.

Plate 60   Japanese Black Pine: Informal style, 1979.

## Japanese Black Pine Informal style

Twelve years old, from seed raised in Surrey. Height 78 cm (2 ft 7 in) spread 68 cm (2 ft 3 in) trunk 5 cm (2 in). Unglazed brown pot, 62 cm (2 ft 1 in) × 45 cm (1½ ft) × 7 cm (3 in).

*Plate 60*. Photographed in 1979. This is the Pine referred to in the section on the Mechanics of Bonsai, which produced nine breaks of bud. The Pine was raised from a batch of seedlings sown in 1967. The seed was from an unknown source but is proving to be a good clone – one that shows good bark and bud characteristics and roots well from cuttings. Prior history: the tree was grown originally (in 1971) in a small flower pot and the roots were checked when the tree was 30 cm (1 ft) in height with a pencil thick trunk. The roots proved to be in an appalling condition and so apart from removing the leading bud, no training was attempted, the tree merely being potted on after root spreading. The bud removal is still apparent as the cause of the swing to the left above the first branch cluster.

1972 (year 5) to 1974 (year 7). In spring 1972 the Pine was transferred into the usual light soil mix. The roots had improved immeasureably and the Pine was a sturdy potential Bonsai. No feeding was carried out. An alternate growth pattern emerged in a 'Y' shape and neither shoot was checked till August. This initial extension of the left hand shoot – the trunk – was misjudged, there is too great an interval between lower and middle tree and earlier pinching would have initiated better taper, which is practically non-existent.

1975 – year 8. The usual cycle of topiary, refinement and placement were not really contributing anything significant until 1975 when it was decided to try a long feeding cycle.

Beginning in January, the tree was moved inside a cold greenhouse and given feed at the rate of a heaped dessertspoon per 60 cm (2 ft) box with a 23 cm (9 in) depth and breadth of 45 cm (1½ ft). The feed was repeated monthly in February and March, fortnightly during April and May, monthly during June and July and reduced by half in August, then left off for that season.

Every emerging shoot that exceeded 5 cm (2 in) was entirely removed and every weaker shoot tip pinched only. The pruning operation was phased gradually and this factor combined with those of fast drainage and the feed supplement necessary to counter the leaching effect of watering schedules inside a greenhouse, all contributed to an amazing cycle of nine separate breaks of bud/shoot removal that began in March, and finished in August when the root production burst the box.

1979 – year 12. The tree potted up to relate the form to the pot in the way a painting is framed before completion. The tree made all the present bulk and trunk diameter in one year and the past four years have been spent refining the forms. When the elements have

**Fig. 68** The same tree in 10 years' time. For explanation of symbols, see text.

been brought back into balance it will be planted out again.

*Fig. 68.* 1990. The tree as it will look in ten years' time. The obvious differences are the extension of branch cluster 'A' which now completely alters the peripheral line, dominating the oval soil area and forming a new base to the triangles described by terminals 'C', 'b1' and 'a'. Motif 'A'–'a' is repeated through 'B'/'b1'–'b2' and echoed in the 'C' complex. In principle, zone 'a' will be developed by a constant expansion of the periphery 'A' as seen in Plate 60. Terminals will first be allowed 5 cm (2 in) of growth before pruning and in alternate years, terminals will be checked at 2.5 cm (1 in) and so on alternately. The extensions will occur outside at the rate of 2½ breaks per year (based on records and conditions in Surrey) and may be further regulated by August pruning.

All other branches are subject to May and August pruning and careful wire arrangement to refine and relieve the breadth and density of 'A'–'a' with a sense of logical increment.

## Mountain Maple Root Over Stone style

Medium stone variant. Quoted age twenty-five years, imported in 1979. Height 53 cm (1 ft 9 in) spread 53 cm (1 ft 9 in) trunk 4 cm (1½ in). Unglazed grey pot, 45 cm (1½ ft) × 35 cm (1 ft 2 in) × 6.25 cm (2½ in).

*Plate 61.* Photographed in 1979. The unit was transferred to this deeper container in summer 1979 when it became apparent the tree was distressed through lack of soil. There was an immediate improvement, the greater available depth of soil providing better rooting and humidifying conditions and contributing a more satisfactory contour.

The right trunk has been appreciably lowered by suspension with covered wire and its laterals spread to establish separate identity and an understructure more harmoniously angled and related to the stone.

Other partially adjusted areas of the tree are the first left and right branches of the left trunk. Previously uptilted, they are being corrected by suspension and lateral spreading, to harmonize with the right trunk, following the principles of the Informal Upright.

Plate 61   Mountain Maple: Root over Stone style, 1979.

Placement on the stone and the roots that grip well, are made still more convincing by the line traceable from the right of the stone, up through the tree. The sensation is of strong, natural growth.

*Fig. 69.* The tree in four to five years. 'A' is now distinct, 'a' has been formed by extending lateral spread and the inner peripheries of 'A–a' have been arranged to harmonize with the contour of the stone. Profiles are broadly domed but straight enough for the natural foliage posture of the species to make pleasing denseness and texture. The width of 'B/C, c' is an obvious reverse of 'A a' and so are 'D' and 'E e'. Occupation and non-occupation, positive and negative are the real strengths of this shape: look at the great potency of the negative areas to the left and to the right under 'A'.

The rock apex and major axial pot limits; upper and lower contours of 'A a' and the terminal triangle of 'E, B and c', may all be thought of as pieces to be juggled. Try making the elements with paper, this will immediately demonstrate the use of space. The technique of paper-masking pictures is a good method of judging the impact of projected pruning – it

Plate 62   Scots Pine: Cascade style, summer 1979.

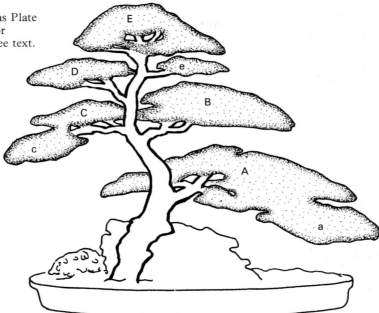

**Fig. 69** The same tree (as Plate 61) in 4–5 years' time. For explanation of symbols, see text.

allows hours of quiet study, days if necessary – and takes much of the indecisive anguish out of imagination, which can be a nerve-wracking business.

## Scots Pine Cascade style

Approximately thirty years old, from a collected tree. Apex to lowest point 68 cm (2 ft 3 in) spread 66 cm (2 ft 2⅜ in) trunk 5 cm (2 in). Unglazed grey pot, 30 cm (12 in) square × 18 cm (7 in) deep.

*Plate 62*. Photographed summer 1979. Prior history 1963. The Pine was collected in spring 1963 as a natural Informal Upright. All major trunk convolutions were naturally formed by the early struggle for survival among old heather stalks.

Until 1977 the tree was grown with others of the same vintage and all were transplanted regularly, given basic pruning, and gradually potted and styled. This tree was the last and one morning after a gale it was found dangling, pot overturned on the bench. The image was obvious and the past fourteen years vanished in wonder at missing what had been seen every day.

The pot was secured sideways to assess the

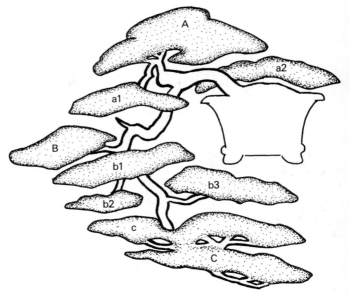

**Fig. 70** The same tree (as Plate 62) in 10 years' time. For explanation of symbols, see text.

**Plate 63**  Saw Leaf Zelkova: Broom style, spring 1979.

new trunk angle and styling was easy, consisting of wire placing the limbs according to Cascade principles but the tricky bit was reversing the foliage. This was accomplished by coiling heavy gauge aluminium wire around branches and twisting each profile through its length, thus avoiding sudden, bark separating creases.

Once styled, the unit was replaced on the shelf the 'right' way up and looked odd! Terminal pruning, feeding and eventually, being forced to grow the tree in the supported dangle position to adjust shoots, made it possible to redevelop and transplant the tree into the present container in spring 1978.

The roots were untangled, spread and pruned and the soil mixture was the standard one. Polythene strings were looped over wires outside the main drainage hole, brought up around and secured over the root ball, further strings being added around the outside. This secured the basic mass and finer placement was achieved after the soil was levelled by the use of a lathe support to prop the lower trunk, still visible at the left base. The unit was placed high up in a shaded greenhouse and watered in well and left strictly undisturbed, and by August 1978 shoots were developed enough to prune but the tree had enjoyed its year of quiet activity. Growth was reasonably vigorous in 1979 – no great shoot length to speak of, but good infilling activity from inner buds, triggered by the 1978 terminal pruning.

The rhythm begins in the right foot of the pot, moves up the side, over the root and through the trunk till it hits that unfortunate trident at mid trunk, then confusion reigns. There is so much of equal diameter, the eye is really misled. The enormous emptiness between apex and lower tree is worrying.

Fig. 71 The same tree in about 5 years' time.

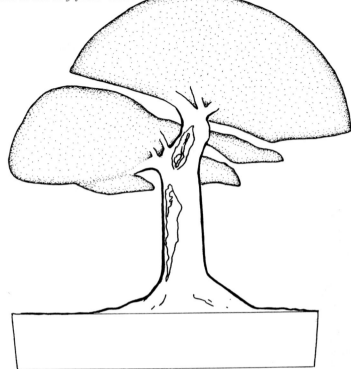

*Fig. 70*. 1990. The tree in ten years. The great differences are in the apparition of 'a1' that has displaced the void and the suppression of 'b2' so the pathway to the 'C' complex is now clear. Broadly, the upper and lower systems are now opposed diamond forms whose major axes meet at the outer terminal of 'B'. Stemming from the root base, the profile and understructure theme is of dome and concavity. The whole shape has a 'comma' formed swing that suits the style.

## Saw Leaf Zelkova Broom style

Quoted age thirty years, imported in 1979. Height 60 cm (2 ft) spread 56 cm (1 ft 10$\frac{3}{8}$ in) trunk 9 cm (3$\frac{1}{2}$ in). Unglazed grey pot, 48 cm (19 cm) × 37 cm (1 ft 4$\frac{3}{4}$ in) × 7.5 cm (3 in).

*Plate 63*. Photographed in spring 1979. The 1978 'offering' picture showed the opposite elevation and made it even more of a lollipop tree. The tree has obviously been trunk chopped, but from the new angle the 'Y' shaped division made by the slanting cut is more acceptable. The cut has been hollowed and casts a shadow in the crutch of the 'Y'.

Lower down, the bark has naturally fallen away and the boundary is marked by a roll of callus. Shortly after this picture was taken, a colony of ants was spotted at the base of the trunk, on investigation the heartwood proved rotten as the ants had been living in the decayed section. After a mini confrontation the decayed section came away; the trunk is now hollow to just below the first left branch.

*Fig. 71*. 1985. The tree in about five years. New grey pot, 54 cm (1 ft 9$\frac{1}{2}$ in) × 33 cm (1 ft 1$\frac{1}{4}$ in) × 13 cm (5 in). The relation between the two heads has remained constant but their 100% extension has now justified the trunk. As the major section develops, the 'Y' shape will disappear with the inward push of the diameter. The trunk will never be the superlative object venerated in immaculate Broom Zelkova but then, neither will they ever give this sensation of survival.

# CONTAINERS

Often defined as the picture frame and hastily passed over, containers as a subject can be as enthralling as the trees, but as a visual study, not a written one. This is where pictorial reference and visual memory, with just enough support from the Basic Criteria section, serves best. So often there is a picture that stimulates a whole chain of allied images but without that key the job is hopeless.

The prime function is of course as a flower pot with unglazed, porous interior, good drainage holes and the rest, but details such as raised drainage holes which cause puddling and mishapen interiors that hold water are often overlooked and lead to root rot. Often these two can be remedied by recontouring the interior with fibreglass or a mixture of bituminous paint and sand.

Apart from basic proportions, muted colours and quiet appearance, there is texture to consider and the patina of the material. It is wise to wait for the design to mature before investing in a special pot that may not ultimately blend or may even jar with the ageing tree. Insight into the subtleties and nuances of the 'right' container and the amalgam of elements necessary to produce that magical gel of tree and pot, does require study, but is immensely rewarding. This is of course for the future and photographs and paper masks with different pot forms and planting angles sketched on them are great aids.

There are other suggestions for the style and shape of the container included in Bonsai Data that reflect the needs of different species.

Suggestions for matching container and styles:

*Formal* – very plain rectangle or oval. Simple linear feet, medium depth.

*Broom* – plain or lipped, shallow to medium rectangle or oval. Simple linear feet.

*Informal* – as above. Sometimes the feet echo some design detail.

*Slanting* – if slender trunked, as for Informal or even Literati, small round. If heavy trunked, a squat, heavy pot that visually counter-balances, or a medium depth plain rectangle or oval. Soft profiles.

*Windswept* – same as for Slanting.

*Semi-Cascade* – deep pots of most forms. The pot should be deep enough for the low branch to clear its base. Try plain pots first.

*Cascade* – as for Semi Cascade except the low branch exceeds the pot depth. Pots with soft profiles are harmonious.

*Literati* – shallow pots, often round and with a rounded section. This continues the literary element: the circle is the void and the earth.

*Driftwood* – if the tree is very lively, a pot that expresses this quality is appropriate. Virtually any harmonious form deep enough to at least equal trunk caliper may be considered. If the tree is static or ponderous, a deep rectangle or oval is used. Detail may be thematic.

*Root over rock* – plain or lipped ovals or rectangles. Simple linear feet. Depth and length are dictated by the variant. Length may follow implied space or the cantilever principle of squatness, or the simple firm base of medium depth.

*Root on rock* – shallow pots rectangles or ovals. Pots are either water vessels or sand receptacles.

*Multi-trunked styles* – all the other styles, from Twin Trunk to Group, may follow the implied space principle, they look well in long ovals or rectangles. Pots can also be as for Literati, or medium depth pots of various shapes can be used.

Texture should harmonise with the tree, nothing cheapens the image more than an old tree in a young-looking or worse still, plastic pot. When colour contrasts are used they are understated. Guard particularly against 'Export Blue' – a debased derivative of the subtlest glaze group, Chun – export blue is only for those whose sensitivity is in the embryo state.

Traditional colour combinations:

*Evergreen* – unglazed ware in brown, red, grey, black and earth-tones – all are muted. May be textured or smooth.

*Deciduous* – as above and also, glazed ware in off-

**Plate 64**   Waterfall stone.

**Plate 65**   Distant mountain stone.

**Plate 66**   Cape stone.

**Plate 67**   House stone.

**Plate 68**   House stone. Also shown in use with
Twin trunk Scots Pine (Colour Plate 20).

**Plate 69**   Bridge stone.

Such stones chosen for their landscape qualities are used separately or in close
association in Bonsai display to suggest mood and place.

white, grey-blue, purple, muddy yellow, blue-green, celadon green.

*Flowering* – as for deciduous.

Guard against strident contrasts and clashes.

## FIBREGLASS ROCK CONSTRUCTION

I developed this technique (see photographs opposite page 88) in 1984 in response to a request from Australia to demonstrate a rock planting. In view of the distance involved, and as I wanted to make one image, I dreamt up this way of manufacturing my preferred shape in a form light enough to carry.

It is important to remember that these rocks give a further dimension to the Bonsai artist's range of facilities. It is easy to make a mistake of pontificating about the use of 'natural' stone only. An aspect of Bonsai that is often missing is basic excitement. In making fibreglass rocks this is very much to the fore and gives enormous pleasure to the creator and observer. The effect is closer to Saikei in feel and spirit, where landscapes are evoked and suggested through the use of assembled rocks and small trees.

## INTERIOR DISPLAY AND PRESENTATION

Bonsai are shown in a manner reminiscent of standards in an art gallery: at the right height; in isolation; against a plain background, devoid of all redundancies such as labels and vulgar little accessories.

HEIGHT Main trees are shown normally with their centre trunk at eye level. Often Bonsai are flanked with a contrast note which may take the form of a grass planting, a stone or subsidiary Bonsai. This constitutes two elements, a third element is permissible in the form of a scroll or equivalent.

Relative scale is vital, no element must conflict with the main Bonsai, placed on a special table chosen for its harmonious quality, or a simple stand, often a polished tree-trunk section.

ISOLATION AND BACKGROUND This is accomplished in Japan by the use of the traditional display alcove or Tokonoma. In the West, display height is governed by whether viewing is more constant from a standing or seated position; whether the tree is displayed in a hallway or lounge, but always mindful of the Tokonoma principle. Backgrounds must be plain and of neutral colour so the viewer may enter the tree and enjoy its design in isolation. Keep 4/5ths of the available space untenanted.

ACCESSORIES Subsidiary accents or trees either blend or contrast with the mood of the main tree but in a way that creates associative images. Scrolls for example, imply connections, and furnish subtle embellishment in their linear quality. They should not be garishly, multi-coloured, or a literal restatement of the mood sought.

PRESENTATION Bonsai must be correctly potted in appropriate, immaculate, ceramic containers. Soil levels and ground covers must be well tended without being obtrusive. All the elements in the tree must be balanced as discussed in the section on Basic Criteria (p. 12). If the tree is presented with wire on it, the wire must be beautifully neat. There are notable examples of what to avoid in the pictorial section on Styles!

Study of Japanese Bonsai exhibition albums will also prove helpful.

## BONSAI DISPLAY, CHELSEA FLOWER SHOW IN LONDON

The sequence of photographs opposite page 89 shows a new type of display that I first used in 1977 incorporating lightweight, high-density polystyrene blocks of differing thicknesses to emulate the feeling of a Tokonoma.

The polystyrene was painted in toning colours using emulsion paints. The tree display stands were made of chipboard, customised for each Bonsai, and painted to match.

# 5 The Pine from native material

Of all the Pines used in Bonsai the Scots Pine is probably the least appreciated. Almost certainly this is because of two factors: lack of stimuli in the absence of pre-trained examples as reference and ignorance of the training potential and versatility of this plant. The best clones of Scots Pine display needle colours which rival the Five Needle Pine in attractiveness and definitely surpass it in vigour. The bark of trees in the south of England is usually very dark and broken into deep fissured rings, while trees from Scotland usually have a lighter bark which gradually darkens and thickens with age. In terms of impressiveness the Scots Pine can be said to fall somewhere between the Five Needle Pine and Black Pine and in Bonsai this presence can be well represented, by careful selection of clone needle colour and bark texture, and by paying meticulous attention to branch 'knuckles' emphasizing the underlying structure and power of planes and trunk.

This Pine also reacts strongly to pruning, as does the Black Pine, provided that one remembers to use always the correct soil and to feed annually on the long cycle basis (p. 146). In those years when the roots have been severely disturbed, one has to be content with little shoot activity and it is bad for the Pine to try to hurry it in this resettlement year. The following year one will reap the benefits of the waiting in a strongly vigorous tree which, with judicious treatment, may well yield as many as three breaks of bud.

The often quoted adage about Pine thickening in the autumn is very true of Scots Pine, so beware! Late summer is a superlative time for grooming, thinning and arranging these trees but do make allowance for the speed at which the wood is bulking up at this season. Constriction in branches can occur in three weeks after wiring for the end of season shape adjustment.

The control of pests is vital and entails careful winter placement which in this context means a well ventilated position where the air is not too humid. High light intensity is mandatory and will help discourage pests. Mealy bugs and woolly aphids are the main problem and frequent attacks can leave unpleasant sooty deposits on foliage and twigs. Routine spraying is obviously sensible and so is changing the nature of the chemical used to avoid the build-up of immunity. A combination of Pyrethrum alternated with a Systemic containing Malathion in a three- to four-week alternation will usually keep the tree clean. Directing a strong water jet through the tree also keeps it clean and helps dislodge the insects.

## Collection

Collecting a natural Scots Pine (Fig. 72) is a wonderful experience and the satisfaction makes the difficulty worthwhile. This difficulty is relative however and the chances of success can be greatly enhanced by first taking a few essentially 'first aid' measures.

Before going on a collecting trip have equal parts of decomposed pine needle litter and coarse sand prepared for instant potting on return. Prepare several large temporary containers – there is no predicting the size or shape of tree or root mass. Erect, if cold greenhouse facilities are not available, a shaded area where the newly potted plant can

**Fig. 72** Pine: collection and early training.
(*a*) The tree as it was found on marshy ground in spring 1973. The branch at midway left appeared to offer pleasing possibilities so the upper right main trunk was cut leaving a stub about 8–10 cm (3–4 in) long for jinning.

(*b*) The tree with the upper trunk removed. The meagre foliage canopy is typical of Pines on wet sites. The bark is characterful and there is an interesting ribbon of sabamiki on the trunk. A circle of ground cover has been removed and the roots have been carefully weeded and checked for fibre.

(*c*) As more than half the top weight of foliage had been removed and as the roots, though sodden were vigorous, the tree was chopped out preserving four to five inches of soil/root depth and a twelve inch diameter. Tools used were a trenching pick with flat spade blade and secateurs. The roots were simply wrapped in plastic for the home trip.

(*d*) The tree as it appeared in autumn 1973. Planted in a wooden box with fast drained establishment soil of 50% pine litter/50% sand. Apart from spreading the roots as far as possible no training has been attempted. After potting in March the tree was allowed a recovery period in a shaded area with foliage sprinkling for a few weeks but as shoots appeared this was phased out. The tree was fed from June onwards.

**Colour Plate 88.** Top: YEAR ONE In summer and autumn, shoots of over 2.5 cm (1 in) are removed. The first diagram shows back budding in response to terminal pruning. Terminal pruning is carried out in August to September and budding can be determined in that year or the following season. I have pruned Pines at this time for the last 30 years with great success. Vital to the formation of back buds is the factor of appropriate feeding. I recommend Cycle 2 and later Cycle 3 (see page 148) in the relevant seasons to support and nourish the tree. It is important not to encourage too vigorous a response. If this is noted later when needles are appearing, be a bit more sparing with the feed.

**Colour Plate 89.** Above: Proof! This is back budding on bare 15 year old wood.

**Colour Plate 90.** Top: YEAR TWO In summer and autumn shoots of over 2.5 cm (1 in) are removed. The second diagram demonstrates needle plucking which is carried out in May/June. The needle/fascicle is preserved at the base and only current year needles are removed. The tree must have a reserve needle on previous years' wood to nourish it while it forms fresh bud. The drawing shows the strange rosettes and fruit-like bud structures produced by the tree in response to this type of wounding. Needles produced in these areas are tiny and witches broom like.

**Colour Plate 91.** Middle: Proof! This close-up shows a typical bud spread produced in response to needle plucking. It is important to observe the summer and autumn shoot removal routines, particularly at the terminals, as otherwise it has been my experience that these inner bud clusters can dry up and abort through being bypassed. Practice needle plucking on no more than $\frac{1}{3}$ to $\frac{1}{2}$ of the overall bulk of needles as this technique will give the tree a bit of a shock.

**Colour Plate 92.** Bottom: YEAR THREE In summer and autumn, shoots of over 2.5 cm (1 in) are removed. The diagram shows the needle reduction and density of growth made possible by this additional end-of-season hard pruning. As I said earlier, I have found autumn trimming to be effective in triggering masses of adventitious buds.

The late Bill Archer showed this method to me of dormant disbudding of Pines. He used the method to promote tiny and dense needles. I modified this technique by the additional cutting into all strong terminal growth with scissors. I usually do this in November and protect from frost and drying winds. Remember it is the combination of the techniques in Years One to Three that produce lasting dwarfness

**Colour Plate 93.** Left: Proof! Next spring and through summer masses of inner and terminal buds are produced.
**Colour Plate 94.** Below: In early summer the back buds are sprouting. See the density!

This sequence shows a Scots Pine undergoing traditional thinning and wiring and then the needle reduction techniques. Notice the effects compounding from year to year.

**Colour Plate 95.** Top: END OF YEAR ONE
The Scots Pine thinned and wired. Primary candles were removed in summer and all longer individual leaves were pulled out. All current year terminal growth was pruned in August and September.

**Colour Plate 96.** Top right: END OF YEAR TWO
One year later. The needles from all latent buds have reduced in size. Little shoot pruning, but considerable thinning was necessary to lighten the form. Needles were plucked in May to July.

**Colour Plate 97.** Above: END OF YEAR THREE
One year later. The density and needle reduction are almost complete. The branch trimming is still to come in November, so most of the needles seen were produced by needle plucking.

**Colour Plate 98.** Right: END OF YEAR FOUR The proof of the system. The new growth has been thinned, trimmed and wired. It is important to thin buds springing from a common point. This relieves the heavy, shrubby appearance found in witches broom cultivars and more importantly, preserves light wood that otherwise would thicken with the extra load.

(*e*) Autumn 1974. The foliage has thickened and there are copious latent buds appearing. The general health of the tree was so good that it was felt shape adjustment might safely be used if of the suspended type. Therefore, friction areas were cushioned with inner tube strips and wires applied to narrow the relevant forks. Other light wires were *loosely* applied to arrange the branches.

(*f*) Autumn 1976. The foliage canopies are beginning to assume a settled outline. Adjustments are being made, this time the head of the tree is being lowered so the tree will display two major foliage levels. The lower branch is being suspended as before and the head is being trained by using a heavy wire former. The tie areas on the trunk were first cushioned with inner tube and then the trunk was carefully secured with heavy plastic sheathed wire.

re-establish. Bottom heat will always help the Pine to root and this can be supplied in a number of ways – the trick here is to keep the foliage moist at all times. If it is at all possible, locate the tree first, ascertain the nature of the soil which will determine the structure of the root and if necessary revisit to take root-corrective measures. This means carrying a small sack of the potting mixture, a trowel and a small trenching pick of the fold-flat type.

Two of the most likely sites for collecting will be wet ground where the Pine seed took root in light peat, and sandy areas, usually where there is a lot of bracken. The wet site is usually the result of a thin soil cover over clay or rock and typically, in the south, the soil is largely a light peat mush deriving in the main from sand, bracken, heather and sedge. The water table rises substantially during winter and spring and it is during the summer that the tree makes its main growth effort. The annual growth is thus compact and were it not for the summer aeration the plant could barely grow at all. The roots of trees found in the wet

site are by and large compact. There is a tendency for the formation of a large tap root but various side anchor roots can be gratifyingly short and the peat area around the trunk often harbours a lot of root fibre. For all these reasons chances of collection from the wet site in one go are favourable, *if* one digs at least one major root out along its length to verify the presence of root fibre. Having tested the root condition, one has to estimate the available amount of root fibre in relation to the weight of the top of the tree and do a little field surgery if necessary, to maintain a sensible balance between foliage and root. If the roots are not good enough, trench around the tree in the standard way and scatter a liberal layer of the potting up mix in and around the root ends after these have been cut. Trees on wet sites rarely have the beneficial Mycorrhiza present in the pine needle litter, as this mould abhors soggy conditions and its introduction can often produce remarkable rooting in a very short time. One then covers the trench over and revisits later – six months for safety. Very possibly rooting may take place in a very few weeks of the trenching operation but it is better for the inexperienced tree fancier to wait for a good solid root pad before lifting.

Pines from sandy sites usually have 'dry feet' but it is the very dryness that produces the tremendously extended roots as they seek water and food. Sand of course is a superb rooting medium and the roots are often fibrous along their entire length. The quality of sand normally dictates the presence of root fibre. If the sand is of the compacted silver type there is usually a fair percentage of rotten bracken in it and other plant litter which does hold moisture and keep roots compact. Not so the Pine rooted into the fine silver sand! It is not uncommon to have two metres or more of root tendrils stretching out radially to an almost unbelievable four metres plus circle.

At home, assess the Pine carefully in terms of available root in relation to the weight of the foliage. The ideal is an equal balance, but the tree will survive without further foliage reduction if available roots are no less than two-thirds of its bulk. All terminals may be reduced or pruned back to adjacent side branches as an added safeguard. If the root ratio should prove inferior, greater reduction of branch length is vital.

Check the temporary container is big enough to accept the root mass when fully spread and that drainage is adequate. Prepare container in the usual way with an ample drainage course and a deep layer of the establishment soil (pine needle and sand). Support the tree while arranging the roots as radially as possible and tie the tree by support strings from nailed wall points, until it feels stable, if necessary using as many guy points as a Big Top – the roots can only benefit. Cushion friction areas with soft material. Add more soil taking it in with the fingers till the roots feel free of air pockets and then pour in more mixture, level off and water in, using vitamin $B_1$ solution over the soil. Water mist the foliage. Remember the cutting syndrome (p. 70) and you will not go far wrong. Spring, rather than late summer, collection is easier to handle in terms of aftercare.

Be guided by the tree: bud activity, maintained needle condition and plumpness of wood are all good portents. Do not be in any hurry to feed – the tree needs its settling in period. If however, the tree seems perky and raring to go, and is producing candles after six to eight weeks, then a gentle feed in July and August with feed 'C' will prove beneficial. Light terminal stopping will help keep growth compact.

The following has been pieced together from notes and records dating from the early fifties. There are detailed techniques of Reduction Pruning as it relates to Collected trees; Development Pruning and finally, Maintenance Pruning on the bench. Every method is the result of the comparison of many exactly parallel situations.

## Reduction pruning

METHOD I

YEAR I This involves the initial cutting into needle bearing terminal wood or total terminal removal to the nearest fork with the object of stimulating inner bud production (Fig. 73a–b). It is also carried out as a routine maintenance technique in August. Backed with the above July and August 'C' feeding, buds will form around the cuts, between needle pairs and in the needled area adjacent to the cut. There *may* also be the odd one or two buds (adventitious buds) appearing at the bases of one and two year old wood and at former cessation points, with or without needles. The significance of this is that Pines prefer to bud in needled areas.

METHOD 2

YEAR 2 If the tree has prominent resting buds of a deep colour and needle colour is also good, feeding may begin in March: cycle 3, feed 'A'.

In May/June the longer candles are reduced by half. Others are tipped and branch terminals are scissor cut in August, retaining two to three pairs of needles (Fig. 74). All terminal and adjacent zone buds will have grown and

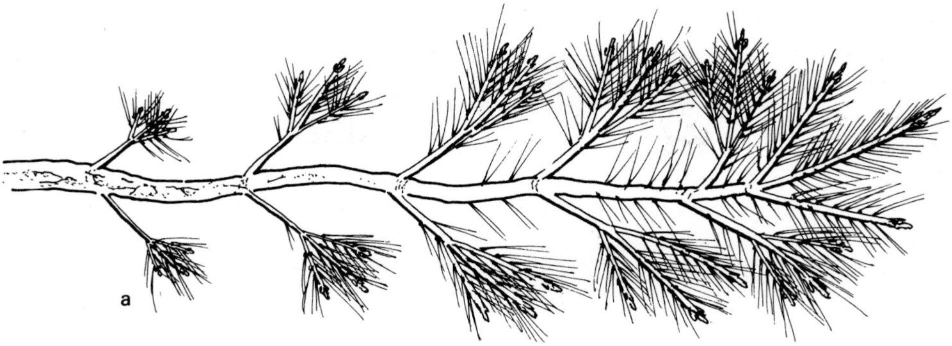

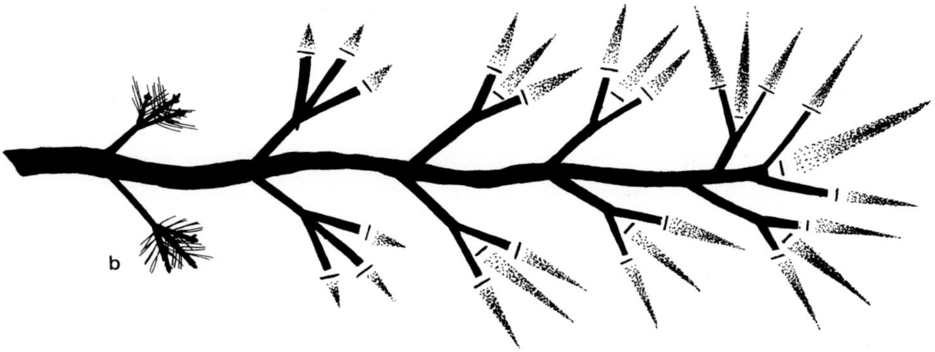

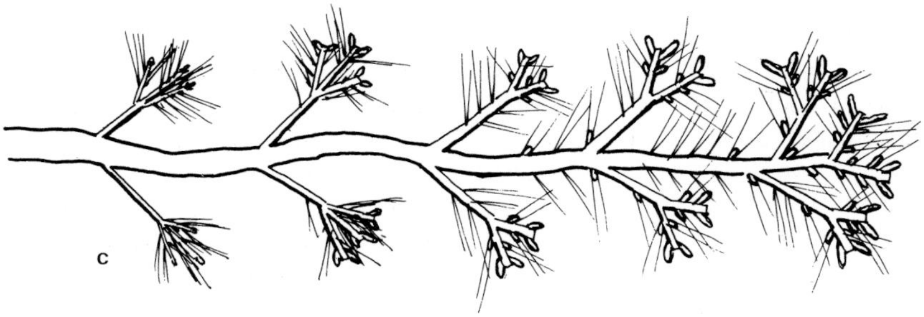

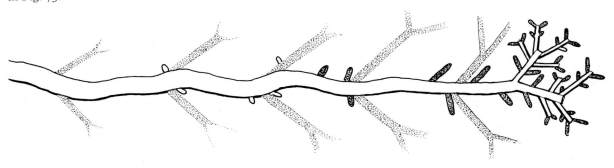

**Fig. 73** Scots Pine: reduction pruning: method 1.
(*a*) Branch before treatment showing overgrown terminals and weak inner branches.
(*b*) Same branch illustrating degree of pruning along the length. (*c*) Bud stimulation as the result of (*b*). Note buds appearing on 1 and 2 year old wood.

**Fig. 74** (*below*)  Scots Pine: reduction pruning: method 2. End of season bud production year 2. All terminals and adjacent zones have been pruned. Note prominence of buds on one and two year old wood and the new buds on 3–4 year old wood. In this diagram, terminal development only is shown for clarity. In fact the proliferation remains in proportion to the rate shown in Fig. 73*c*.

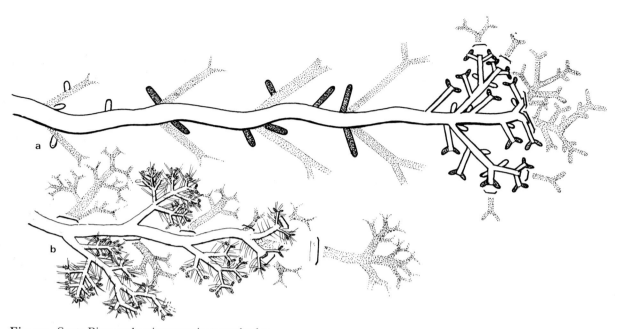

**Fig. 75**  Scots Pine: reduction pruning: method 3.
(*a*) End of season bud production year 3, showing the results of outer candles and longer adventitious shoots. Reduction of outer terminal areas is carried out to strengthen the new inner activity. Note that adventitious buds are now appearing on 4–5 year old wood. (*b*) After a number of seasons when inner branches are developed, the opposite branching pattern is discouraged. Note the vigour achieved on 4–5 year old wood compared to Fig. 73*a*.

been pruned. These in their turn will have formed buds in their terminal areas and so on.

The adventitious buds that appeared at the bases of one and two year old wood will be at half matchstick length, and matchhead stages of prominence respectively. Look for adventitious bud breaks on still older wood.

METHOD 3
YEAR 3 Check bud and needle colour in December of Year 2. If good, commence cycle 1, feed 'A' (the long cycle) in January of Year 3. In May all longer, outer candles are removed completely and others reduced by half, including the longer of the outer adventitious shoots (Fig. 75).

By August, further deep pruning may be possible depending on the vigour and further apparition of adventitious buds.

The treatments of Year 2 and Year 3 are alternated except for the feeding cycle, which remains at cycle 1, feed 'A', until the branch length/inner growths are acceptable.

## Development pruning

METHOD 4
YEAR 1 This works best on stock needing increased thickness of trunk planted in huge containers. It is only used on healthy, well established trees.

Commence cycle 1, feed 'A' and alternate with feed 'B', given weekly over foliage – this will increase the growth rate.

Delay pruning till August, by this time the trunk terminal should be at least 60 cm (2 ft) long. Prune trunk terminal at base making the cut away from the viewing side. All branch terminals in the upper tree are removed completely and reduced by half in the lower tree (Fig. 76). This technique increases trunk diameter but is tough on trained branches, particularly low ones.

METHOD 5
YEAR 2 Commence cycle 1, feed 'A' only. Just tip candles that exceed 5 cm (2 in). Year 1

pruning initiates bud breaks around the cuts and extensively through the needled zones and it is vital not to overstrain the tree by further deep pruning. Look for adventitious bud breaks on wood of up to seven years and older.

## METHOD 6

YEAR 3 Commence cycle 1, feed 'A' and alternate with feed 'B' given weekly over foliage. Completely remove all candles that exceed 2.5 cm (1 in), phasing this operation through the season to minimize shock. By August, the primary candles will have largely been replaced with secondary candles, in whorls of three to five shoots (Fig. 77). These are trimmed, retaining enough shoot length to bear two to three pairs of leaves and this will produce further buds near terminal areas.

Fig. 76 (*left*) Scots Pine: development pruning: method 4.
Note trunk thickening and the relative severity of pruning. For details, see text.

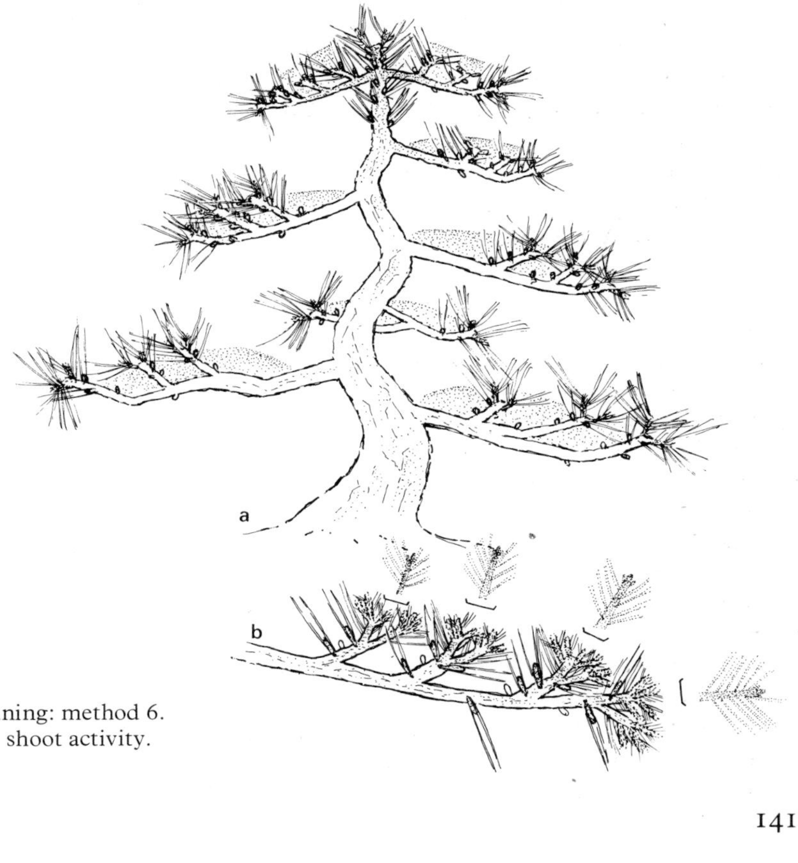

Fig. 77 Scots Pine: development pruning: method 6.
(*a*) End of season bud production and shoot activity.
(*b*) Maintenance pruning.

**Plate 70** Collected Scots Pine in the second year of Method 6 development.

Any leaves that exceed desirable length may be plucked from their sheath before they harden, if in so doing the tree is not robbed of more than 50% of current growth. Strange rosettes of buds often appear as a result, either in the current or following season. This pseudo witches broom is interesting but usually aborts after a year or two, but meanwhile needle lengths in the treated zones are much reduced, and adventitious buds are freely produced.

Pruning variations should be used according to age of material. Pines up to twenty years old will accept Methods 1 to 6 but they are not really happy with Method 4. Older Pines may be badly affected by Method 4 and may need more than one recuperative year. There is bound to be tremendous variation and pruning must be based on observation of the individual tree and not mechanics.

WIRING Trees are wired in August following standard practice. Check frequently for wire constriction, particularly during the feed 'C' time-zone, August to October, and even after a week!

CONTAINERS Scots Pine flourish in medium to deep containers because these remain evenly damp. Shallower containers, used where appropriate to style, need special care for moisture maintenance and it is advisable in such cases to mound the soil or provide protection during hot sun and windy periods.

With well established trees, it is possible to reduce new needle length by monitoring the water ration. The trees are never allowed to become bone-dry, and careful daily probing is vital to ascertain how far drying has progressed – if the soil feels more than 30% dry by depth, water must be given *immediately*. The process is commenced when Pine buds lengthen, through candle development and till needle set – about March to June. It must be remembered that this is a process requiring minutely observed judgement and factors of extra sun and wind must be allowed for, otherwise the tree loses too much moisture, dehydration and sun-scorch ensues and die-

Year 2 needle-borne buds, depending on terminal adjacency, will either have made sufficient length to tip prune, or be at half matchstick prominence. Remove central buds from branch terminals by fingernail picking, to prevent too much growth in the following season. Repeat the three yearly cycle of Methods 4 to 6, until trunk diameter is established.

## Maintenance pruning
Follow Method 6 treatment but omit foliar feeding with 'B'. In August of every other year, branch terminals are trimmed back to the nearest side branch which is then wired into position. Vertical shoots, overcrowded shoots, overdense needles and hanging shoots or foliage are all pruned. Depending on the type of bud production and needle profile desired, the tree may be lightened by removing the lower, older needles on each shoot, but bear in mind needle presence assists bud breaks.

back can result. The micro-climate, idiosyncracies of the tree, the pot and the soil must all be taken into account before trying the technique. However, if it is properly carried out, no damage is caused and needle length can be brought down to 1.25 cm ($\frac{1}{2}$ in). Standard watering schedules are resumed after June to July as needle and candle length will then be set.

SOIL The mixture, based on its own litter of rotted pine needles is ideal for the Scots Pine and its variants. Through the use of this soil root initials have been produced on Scots Pine from very old bark. As this Pine is virtually impossible to root, this discovery is of some significance. As with all Pines, drainage must be rapid but the Scots Pine grows best in a steady dampness – extremes should be avoided. Mycorrhizal fungus, the benevolent white mould called mycelium, and beloved of Pine roots, is incorporated naturally in such a mixture and soil dampness is conducive to its rapid spread. Others using the recommended mixture either in pots or growing beds report equal success, and the reports have been consistently favourable over many years.

REPOTTING The Pine is transplanted in March/April and presents no great problem, the suggested soil making all the difference to rapid re-establishment. Aftercare is standard. August repotting is possible but greenhouse facilities must be available for over-wintering.

VARIANTS Scots Pine cultivars: Beuvronensis and Watereri are among the best Yatsubusa forms for Bonsai, *if* sufficient allowance is made for the strong reaction of both trees to root disturbance. The following year can be very off-putting even with fine healthy stock. Unfortunately, as most of the available material is root-bound, there have been some bad experiences.

Once established however, both cultivars are wonderful. The rule is strictly: no regular pruning schedules until Year 2 after root disturbance. Methods 1 to 3 may be necessary with overgrown stock. A modified version of

Method 6 works for maintenance pruning: shoots are not totally removed. Combined with the genetic dwarfing habit, this pruning provokes great bud activity and adventitious bud breaks on one to five year old wood and needle length is reduced. The rough bark, needle and bud colour, and twig detail of both cultivars are very promising and will yield classic Bonsai in the future.

## THREE YEAR NEEDLE LENGTH REDUCTION CYCLE FOR ESTABLISHED SCOTS PINE

Comparisons with witches broom cultivar needle lengths and those of the normal Scots Pine, showed that even after some years of routine pine culture, the dwarf strains were still superior in terms of compact needle size, although definitely no match for the wild Scots Pine in general vigour and happiness in a pot. I decided to pass on a method that evolved from these tests and suggest that as a quick way of tidying and maintaining foliage texture on the normal Scots Pine without undue stress to the tree.

The pruning system harnesses the fantastic response that Scots Pine has to pruning; it produces a false witches broom almost in effect by maximising bud production and thereby reducing the needle length as the energy is dissipated through all the extra growth points. I first worked on this idea in the late 1950s and others have fairly recently applied it to established Scots Pines, with interesting results.

Unless the tree is solidly established and has been potted for at least four years, this technique will not really work as it is a refinement only process. Younger or recently potted trees have such strength that any needle reduction will be minimal or of short duration.

# 6 General care

## Placement

Bonsai are grown outdoors on shelves elevated to viewing height. In winter alternative placement is necessary to avoid direct frost. On very exposed sites it is worth rigging wind baffle-plates round the shelving but sun protection is rarely necessary in the UK.

The Bonsai shelving illustrated follows the usual pattern. Piles are formed of three to four concrete building blocks mortared together to give viewing height, on footings secured in the usual way. 15 cm (6 in) × 5 cm (2 in) wooden cross members were fastened across the piles and then spaced shelving of 13 cm (5 in) × 5 cm (2 in) planks were fitted and nailed down. The timber was weather proofed (*Plate 71*).

The Nursery in Surrey faces due south so the trees have day long sun exposure. In warm weather or when prevailing winds blow, watering becomes necessary twice a day, morning and evening, after sundown. The slatted shelving permits air passage round the trees and promotes good health, deterring mildew attacks and bugs that prosper in stagnant air.

Full sun exposure strengthens the trees and partially retards growth. There is a tendency for the foliage of Bonsai in full sun to be yellower than those in light shade. This is simply a case of the plant availing itself of certain bands of its available pigmentation range rather than all, and is quite natural. Elevate Cascade trees and secure them to the bench with string. Any newly potted or top-heavy plants are also tied.

*Winter Placement.* Clear polythene curtains are fixed from the sides of the shelves ready to be draped to the ground and the Bonsai are placed under the shelves, just resting on the shingle. No losses were sustained during the very severe winter of 1978/79, when very low temperatures were recorded daily for some weeks. If the trees had remained in the wind while frozen they would certainly have been killed. The wind takes moisture out of the tree – the frozen roots cannot redress the balance and if the cycle continues the tree dies through freeze-drying. The light film curtains prevent direct frost and wind passage and therefore the trees remain in good condition and colour. The colour of frost-nipped Pines or Junipers can be alarming but is usually not serious if protection is forthcoming and will disappear in the spring. Frost discolouration occurs as yellow tipped needles or as general greying or mauving of the foliage. Soil also plays its part in overwintering; if it is correctly balanced and light, there will be no winter root damage. During winter, trees are stored away giving evergreens more available light than deciduous subjects. As spring bud activity starts, the less well-lit trees need more light to prevent damage. Trees under slatted shelves usually remain wet in winter and seldom, if ever, need water but it is sensible to check regularly. Trees overwintered under cover need to remain cool, well lit and ventilated, and should be watered approximately every two weeks. Winter dehydration is not common in the UK but it can happen. In spring, trees are replaced on the shelves, keeping a watchful eye for frosts and strong winds. The leaves of deciduous subjects will need protection until fully out and 'leather hard' to the touch.

**Plate 71** · General view of the nursery shelving.

## Watering

As growth extends there is a universal change from the winter soil condition, every pot is suddenly dry as roots become active once again. Roots need even moisture and watering is always based on this but allowance must be made for season, micro-climate and the endearingly unpredictable UK weather, so do not be mechanical – learn from the tree.

The process is to water the soil with a fine rain till the surplus drips from the drainage holes. In hot or windy weather this is repeated after about ten minutes. Foliage spray is beneficial after sundown. Check for the need to water by using the fingers as a moisture gauge and by pinching the soil between thumb and fore-finger. If the soil powders it is too dry; if it holds and rolls it is just right; if it squelches – be careful!

The nature of the water used is really determined by getting a pH analysis. Some areas have a very alkaline tap water, but in Surrey for example, any alkalinity is more than compensated for by the use of our slightly acidic potting soils. Storage of tap water over a few days neutralizes it and the Japanese make a decorative feature of the water tank – just a thought! General drought or dry periods can produce yellowing of foliage or even sun-scorch. Young growth on evergreens can be permanently discoloured but luckily most deciduous subjects usually shed the damaged leaves and produce a second crop.

## Feeding

Normally only carried out from bud activity to August each year, feeding cycles and types vary according to the age, species and location when potted and is varied when trees are being developed. Older trees are generally fed with less nitrogen and in lesser amounts than younger trees. Older trees are the subject of detailed refinement that is easily lost, while youngsters are definitely in the broad brush band of treatment. Both comments must be qualified by adding that older Bonsai are often dangerously underfed in the effort to preserve detail, while young trees which have reached desired trunk diameter, no longer need that heavy feeding which threatens planned taper.

Suggested feeds found among the most effective in records kept over the last ten years, are those classified as 'A' and 'B', both these may be duplicated fairly easily, but 'C' is critical. The main feeds are classified as 'A', 'B' and 'C' and not by their brand names to avoid problems should manufacturers change any analysis.

Analysis:

|  | Nitrogen | Phosphorous | Potash |
|---|---|---|---|
| Feed A | 6.5 | 7.7 | 5 |
| Feed B | 10 | 10 | 27 |
| Feed C | 0 | 10 | 10 |

Dosage rates: Feed 'A', half a teaspoon of granules sprinkled on soil surface of a 15 cm (6 in) pot with 5 cm (2 in) depth is the correct rate; preserve this rate proportionally according to pot size. Feed 'B', diluted to manufacturers directions and given as abundantly as water when applied; Feed 'C', applied at a dilution of one part/six hundred parts of water, applied in the same fashion as feed 'B'.

APPLICATIONS Pines overwintered under cover may be put on a long feed cycle; Two Needle Pines are put on long feed cycle 1, monthly from January to March. If development is planned, lighter applications are given at two week intervals from April to July, when they terminate. For Five Needle Pines, and just for maintenance of Two Needle Pines, only feed at half rate during January to March and monthly till July, cycle 2. Feed 'C' is given monthly after both cycles from August to October.

Other conifers are fed by the rate of cycle 2 but the cycle is shorter, beginning in March – this is cycle 3. Cycle 3 may employ either 'A' or 'B' or use them alternately, feed 'C' follows in August to October. The roots of conifers are slightly active in winter so the long cycle is safe.

Feed 'A' depends on warmth for its interaction so is used in cycle 1 in protected conditions, Pines definitely prefer its slower action. Feed 'B' is a good spur and all-round feed and feed 'C' helps ripen and harden plant tissue.

DECIDUOUS SPECIES Feeding is started with established trees when buds begin to open. It is unsafe to feed before as roots of deciduous subjects will be damaged – feeding is based on observation rather than a mechanical time reference. All species should be kept as cool as possible during winter and any plants that sprout early (mid-February is early in Surrey) may be fed with 'C' fortnightly till mid-March. This will strengthen the tree without encouraging early growth that can be frost-nipped.

In normal years at first bud, deciduous subjects are fed with 'B', twice a week for two weeks, then weekly for three weeks, then fortnightly, but alternating every other week with feed 'A' – this is cycle 4. Terminate in July and feed monthly with 'C' in August and September. Cycle 4 spurs the tree and the rates must be regulated according to age. 'C' hardens the growth and helps diameter.

FLOWERING SPECIES Feeding begins with leaf activity and trees are fed with 'C' fortnightly for six weeks or till flowering starts. Feed every other week with 'B' if leaves are yellow. Do not feed during flowering. Do not feed larger fruiting trees such as Crab Apple till fruit are well developed.

Recommence feeding after fruit size or flowering is achieved, using 'A' and 'B' alternately every ten days till July/August. Feed with 'C' monthly from August to October – cycle 5. Cycle 5, with the use of 'C', builds the necessary reserves in the plant for flowering and fruiting.

No tree is fed within one month of repotting. Problems commonly occur with Satsuki Azalea that does not care for feed 'A', and Japanese Five Needle Pine that likes small amounts of whatever feed is used. Excessive doses with either species are fatal.

With the exception of cycle 1, suggested cycles assume regular outdoor placement and well-drained soil. Obviously there are variable factors, but if observation is the main guide, sound growth should be maintained by following the principles outlined.

Always make sure the soil is damp prior to feeding otherwise feed scorch is inevitable.

## Pest and disease control

APHIDS Grey-black or green bulbous insects that secrete a sticky substance called Honeydew beloved by ants. Aphids infest most species and even invade the roots, particularly of Pines. They are best treated by alternated spraying with Systemics and Pyrethrum. Root aphids may be treated by removing the Bonsai from the pot and applying Systemic spray directly to the root ball. Cleanse the pot interior. All treatments require mild solutions. Repeat foliage applications on a routine two to three week basis. Root aphids are checked and sprayed against in Spring and August. Spraying on a regular basis from bud activity to August will keep trees clean. Over winter check for any aphids on densely foliaged subjects like Needle Juniper or Pines and spray if necessary.

CATERPILLARS These can appear in mid-

## FEEDING  Coniferous Trees  Cycle 1

| | JAN | FEB | MAR | APR | MAY | JUN | JUL | AUG | SEP | OCT | NOV | DEC |
|---|---|---|---|---|---|---|---|---|---|---|---|---|
| Feed A Fisons 'GH5' | 1 | 1 | 1 | 1 | 1 | 1 | 1 | | | | | |
| Feed C Fisons Flower and Fruit developer 0–10–10 Tomorite is an acceptable substitute | | | | | | | | 1 | 1 | 1 | | |

| | JAN | FEB | MAR | APR | MAY | JUN | JUL | AUG | SEP | OCT | NOV | DEC |
|---|---|---|---|---|---|---|---|---|---|---|---|---|
| DEVELOPMENT STAGE | | | | 2 | 2 ½ strength | 2 | 2 | | | | | |
| Feed A | 1 | 1 | 1 | | | | | | | | | |
| Feed C | | | | | | | | 1 | 1 | 1 | | |

## FEEDING  Coniferous Trees  Cycle 2

| | JAN | FEB | MAR | APR | MAY | JUN | JUL | AUG | SEP | OCT | NOV | DEC |
|---|---|---|---|---|---|---|---|---|---|---|---|---|
| Feed A ½ strength | 1 | 1 | 1 | 1 | 1 | 1 | 1 | | | | | |
| Feed C | | | | | | | | 1 | 1 | 1 | | |

# FEEDING  Coniferous Trees  Cycle 3

| | JAN | FEB | MAR | APR | MAY | JUN | JUL | AUG | SEP | OCT | NOV | DEC |
|---|---|---|---|---|---|---|---|---|---|---|---|---|
| Feed A Fisons 'GH5' | | | I | | I | | I | | | | | |
| Feed B 'Phostrogen' | | | | I | | I | | | | | | |
| Feed C Fison '0–10–10' or Tomorite | | | | | | | | I | I | I | | |

# FEEDING  Deciduous Trees  Cycle 4

| | MAR | APR | MAY | JUN | JUL | AUG | SEP |
|---|---|---|---|---|---|---|---|
| Feed A | | I I I | I I I | I I | I | | |
| Feed B | 2 2 I I I | I I I | I I I | I I I | I | | |
| Feed C | | | | | | I | I |

# FEEDING  Flowering Trees  Cycle 5

| | MAR | APR | MAY | JUN | JUL | AUG | SEP | OCT |
|---|---|---|---|---|---|---|---|---|
| Feed A Fison 'GH5' | | | | I I I | I I I I | | | |
| Feed B Phostrogen | If leaves are yellow I I I | | | I I | I I I | I | | |
| Feed C Fisons '0–10–10' or Tomorite | I I I I I | | | | | I | I | I |

season and the spray schedules outlined above will eliminate them.

EARTHWORMS Placement on elevated shelves will prevent their entry. If wormcasts appear on the soil surface, check the root mass when the season permits and remove the culprits – they usually surface when disturbed.

MEALY BUGS AND WOOLLY APHIDS Like white blobs of cotton wool and areas of cigarette ash respectively. The treatment is as for aphids. If the regular schedules fail, Emulsion Sprays or Malathion will take care of the situation. Remember to dilute the dosage. Blast the foliage with water regularly to wash away the corpses. Painting with Methylated Spirits will take out limited attacks. Pines, Beech and Apples can be badly hit. The effects of infestation on Apples are cankerous looking lumps and these should be pared away after treatment and painted with tree seal. Pines can be greatly debilitated by these pests.

MILDEW Discoloured patches mainly confined to trunk and foliage. Correct placement with adequate ventilation are the factors that counter this disease and allied conditions, which begin with high humidity, poor air circulation through leaves and soil, combined with warmth. Leaf spotting is usually a virus introduced by aphids and aggravated by the use of heavy soil – Trident Maple is often badly effected. Trees affected by mildew are treated by restored ventilation through better placement and leaf reduction to dry the air around the tree by increased flow, the removal of all damaged foliage, and finally, spraying with Systemic Fungicide or Bordeaux Mixture. Heavy soil may be offset to some extent by reduced watering until it may be safely changed from August onwards to spring. Protect tree if a soil change is necessary.

NEMATODES OR EELWORMS Presence indicated by warty growths on roots. Check for these in spring or in August if any Rosaceous plant behaves oddly with sudden foliage wilt.

Plate 72 Wheels and concentration are needed to move the larger Bonsai!

The growths are sliced off and Systemic Fungicide applied before sealing the cuts. Treatment may be continued quite naturally by total soil removal and replanting the subject in a soil mixture high in Mycorrhizal activity such as the pine needle mix already suggested. The humus content produces other eelworms which eat the nasties and fungal Mycelium which actually produces loops that trap and destroy the eelworms.

On the subject of Mycorrhizal fungal activity: care should be taken not to confuse the *frills* of Mycelium which are a yellow-white when healthy, and positively beneficial, with the blue-white root cover generated by root aphid. If unsure, check with a lense, the aphids show as distinct round bodies.

RED SPIDER Largely taken care of by the

routine spraying. They love dry conditions so water misting is a good prophylactic. If these tiny red mites do get a hold they will discolour evergreen foliage dreadfully.

ROOT ROT The recommended schedules for repotting, soils, placement, watering and feeding, combined with common sense will hopefully make this condition a thing of the past.

The signs, which appear in the spring are very weak shoot extension, combined with dehydration wrinkles in the bark. Treatment consists of removing outer soil and planting in a temporary container with very sandy light soil. Water the plant in, soil only, with vitamin $B_1$ transplant solution. Mist foliage with water regularly but keep the roots on the dry side. Treat it as a cutting. If the condition is not too far advanced and is treated without delay, it should recover.

SCALE INSECT Treat with dormant Emulsion Sprays or remove by hand. These are pod-like insects on twigs and branches. Rosaceous plants and surprisingly, Yews, are badly affected.

NEEDLE CAST Affecting Scots Pine. Areas of leaves become spangled with yellow and orange bands which in later stages of the disease display characteristic black spots (fruiting bodies) along the needle wall. Patches of needles lose colour and die and drop.

Needle cast may be treated with a contact spray containing copper fungicide. The solution may be applied at two week intervals as a foliar spray during the growing season and in dormancy, if the weather is mild. Remove and burn all discoloured needles from the tree and soil surface.

## Tools

There are certain tools which are indispensable in the creation of Bonsai. Illustrated (Plate 32) are a typical range in daily use, described clockwise from top left they are:

MEDIUM SIZE CLAMP Described in the sec-

tion on Wiring, (p. 88) this push-pull clamp will happily shift wood of 2.5 cm (1 in) in diameter.

GENERAL PURPOSE SHEARS These long bladed shears enable even cuts to be made over a broad area and are ideal for repotting.

SMALL CLAMP A daintier version of that described above, this is used for making precise and limited bends in heavier grade limbs where wiring is awkward.

JIN PLIERS These are used in bark stripping and have knurled interfaces that bite into the strips, saving thumbnails.

WIRE CUTTERS, LARGE Available in several sizes, these cutters slice right to their points and exert incredible leverage.

FINE PRUNING SCISSORS Used in detailed work, such fine blades are reserved for twigs of up to matchstick diameter.

LONG-HANDLED SCISSORS Used as above but the extra length eases entry into confined areas.

BRANCH CUTTERS The slanted blades make immaculate concave cuts and are used for heavier branch removal and fork pruning, their clean action usually obviating further wound cleansing.

A minimum short list would be: general shears, branch cutters, fine pruning scissors and wire cutters. A turntable for considering the tree at different angles when training is a very useful and easily made item.

## Conclusion

I hope the outlined descriptions and methods will be found stimulating. Because understanding frees, there is no substitute for the joy of basic study and the promotion of visual memory as a means of bringing the student to the point of original design. Traditional art training calls for intensive study which paradoxically generates true creative energy and that it seems to me is worth having.

# Appendix: cultural data

# Cultural Data

| Species | Type and features | Repotting | Soil. Standard mix | Watering | Feeding | Branch pruning |
|---|---|---|---|---|---|---|
| **EVERGREEN TREES** | | | | | | |
| **Cedar** | Fine needles, flattened branches | Mar./Apr. Every 2–5 yr according to age | Good drainage | Evenly moist & spray foliage | Cycle 3, feed A & B | March & August |
| **Cryptomeria** | Fine green needles, shaggy bark | Mar./Apr. Every 2–5 yr according to age | Good drainage | Plenty of foliage water. Abhors dry air | Cycle 3, feed A & B | March & August |
| **Cypress** | Fine green frilled sprays. Shaggy bark | Mar./Apr. Every 2–5 yr according to age | Good drainage | Plenty of foliage water. Abhors dry air | Cycle 3, feed A & B | March & August |
| **Juniper, Chinese. Also Blaauws Juniper** | Cordlike foliage often features Shari & Jin | Mar./Apr. Every 2–5 yr according to age | Some extra lime is helpful. Try limestone drainage course | Evenly moist & spray foliage | Cycle 3, feed A & B | March & August |
| **Juniper, Needle. Also Common Juniper** | Gorselike foliage with white stomatic band | Mar./Apr. Every 2–5 yr according to age | Good drainage | Plenty of foliage water. Abhors dry air | Cycle 3, feed A & B | March & August |
| **Pine, Japanese Black** | 2 needle. Rough bark and dark needles | Mar./Apr. Every 2–5 yr according to age | Good drainage | Evenly moist & spray foliage | Cycle 1, feed A | March & August |
| **Pine, Japanese Black var. 'Corticata'. Also Japanese Red Pine & Mugo Pine** | As above. Widely extended slabbed wings of bark | Mar./Apr. Every 2–5 yr according to age | Good drainage | Evenly moist & spray foliage | Cycle 2, feed A | March & August |
| **Pine, Japanese five needle** | White stomatic band gives foliage silvery appearance | Mar./Apr. Every 2–5 yr according to age | Good drainage | Evenly moist & spray foliage | Cycle 2, feed A | March & August |
| **Spruce, Ezo. Also Alberta Spruce etc.** | Neat foliage in rounded bundles. Darkish bark rough with age | Mar./Apr. Every 2–5 yr according to age | Good drainage | Plenty of foliage water | Cycle 2, feed A | March & August |
| **Yew. Also Podocarpus** | Dark green foliage, fissured bark | Mar./Apr. Every 2–5 yr according to age | Good drainage | Evenly moist & spray foliage. Cannot stand soggy soil | Cycle 3, feed A & B | March & August |
| **DECIDUOUS TREES** | | | | | | |
| **Beech** | Lanceolate leaves. Silver grey bark. Retains old foliage over Winter | Mar./Apr. Every 2–3 yr according to age & vigour | Good drainage plus some expanded clay or *good* loam | Standard | Cycle 4, feed B & A | Aug/Sept |

| Pruning shoots | Wiring | Growing season placement | Dormant season placement | Pests | Containers |
|---|---|---|---|---|---|
| Prune back soft shoots continually. When old branches are cut, prune twigs less | Aug. through Winter, use covered wires | Light shade | Early frost protection mandatory | Relatively free | Deep oval or rectangle. Likes root run |
| As for Needle Juniper. Abhors metal contact so limit scissor pruning to grooming | Aug. through Winter, use covered wires | Light shade | Frost protection particularly after pruning | Spray with systemic fungicide for blight | Medium depth oval or rectangle. Likes root run. |
| Nip extending frills or sprays. Clean out interiors | Aug. through Winter | Light shade | Frost protection particularly after pruning | Relatively free | Elegant ovals & rectangles |
| Pinch off tips of primary & secondary shoots & so on with thumb & forefinger. Deeper pruning induces juvenile growth | Aug. through Winter | Light shade | Frost protection particularly after pruning | Red spider | Elegant ovals & rectangles |
| As for Chinese Juniper. Lower branches need ample light | Aug. through Winter | Light shade | Frost protection particularly after pruning | Aphids | Elegant ovals & rectangles |
| According to age & evolution. Method 6 | Aug. through Winter | Full sun | Frost protection particularly after pruning | Aphids, mealy bug & red spider | Chunky rectangle or oval |
| Method 5. Terminals are tipped in Aug. every other year | Aug. through Winter | Full sun | Frost protection particularly after pruning | Aphids, mealy bug & red spider | Very heavy rectangles & ovals rough textures |
| Method 5. Terminals are tipped in Aug. every other year | Aug. through Winter | Full sun | Frost protection particularly after pruning | Aphids, mealy bug & red spider | Lighter rectangles & ovals to harmonize with more feminine appearance |
| Twist foliage sprouts off with thumb & forefinger when 1.25–2.5 cm (½–1 in) in length. Phase over 3–4 weeks | Do not twist unduly | Watch for sun scorch | Frost protection particularly after pruning | Aphids, mealy bug & red spider | As for Black Pine |
| Prune back soft shoots continually. When old branches are cut, prune twigs less | Aug. through Winter, use covered wires | Light shade | Early frost protection mandatory | Scale | Deep oval or rectangle. Likes root run |
| Soft pruning, taking all but 2 leaves. Trim back in Aug. Branches may be developed by hard pruning technique | June. Covered wires | Light shade, burns easily | Early frost protection mandatory | Aphids, mealy bug & scale | Medium depth; oval or rectangle |

# Cultural Data

| Species | Type and features | Repotting | Soil. Standard mix | Watering | Feeding | Branch pruning |
|---|---|---|---|---|---|---|
| **Birch, Silver** | Lanceolate leaves. Silver white bark | Mar./Apr. Every 2–3 yr according to age & vigour | Good drainage plus some expanded clay or *good* loam | Drench | Cycle 3, feed A. Too much Nitrogen inhibits silver bark formation | Aug/Sept |
| **Elm, Chinese** | Lanceolate leaves, smaller than Zelkova. Ridged bark like Scots Pine | Mar./Apr. Every 2–3 yr according to age & vigour | Standard soil | Standard | Cycle 4, feed B & A | March or August |
| **Ginkgo** | Bi-lobed leaves. Primitive appearance. Coarse buff bark | Mar./Apr. 1–3 yr according to age | Good drainage plus some expanded clay or *good* loam | Drench | Cycle 4, feed B & A | Aug/Sept |
| **Hornbeam** | Lanceolate leaves. Silver buff striped bark. Retains old foliage over Winter | Mar./Apr. Every 2–3 yr according to age & vigour | Good drainage plus some expanded clay or *good* loam | Drench | Cycle 4, feed B & A | March or August |
| **Larch** | Starry green leaves, buff grey bark | Mar./Apr. 1–3 yr according to age | Standard soil | Even moisture & foliage spray | Cycle 4, feed B & A | March & dormancy |
| **Maple, Mountain** | Green palmate leaves, silvery bark, red Autumn colour | Mar./Apr. Every 2–3 yr according to age & vigour | Good drainage | Even moisture & spray foliage | Cycle 4, feed B & A | July & August |
| **Maples, Rough-barked** | Arakawa, corky dotted areas like liquid amber. Itsusai Nishiki, the Pine bark Maple, ridged bark like Pseudo Acacia | Mar./Apr. Every 2–3 yr according to age & vigour | Good drainage | Even moisture & spray foliage | Cycle 4, feed B & A | July & August |
| **Maple, cvs. 'Seigen' 'Chishio' & 'Deshojo'** | Flushes flamingo pink/summer red & green/red in Autumn. Silver bark | Mar./Apr. Every 2–3 yr according to age & vigour | Good drainage | Even moisture & spray foliage | Cycle 4, feed B & A | July & August |
| **Maple, 'Yatsubusa' cvs. 'Kyohime' (green form) & red forms e.g. 'Beni-maiko'** | Tiny features throughout & silvery bark | Mar./Apr. Every 2–3 yr according to age & vigour | Good drainage | Even moisture & spray foliage | Cycle 4, feed B & A | July & August |
| **Maple, Trident** | 3 lobed leaves, buff grey bark, flaking to orange. Twigs darken with age. Good rooting structure. Red Autumn colour | Mar./Apr. Every 2–3 yr according to age & vigour | Good drainage | Even moisture & spray foliage | Cycle 4, feed B & A | July & August |
| **Zelkova** | Lanceolate, saw edged leaves. Silver grey bark & fine twigs | Mar./Apr. Every 2–3 yr according to age & vigour | Good drainage plus some expanded clay or *good* loam | Drench | Cycle 4, feed B & A | March or August |

| Pruning shoots | Wiring | Growing season placement | Dormant season placement | Pests | Containers |
|---|---|---|---|---|---|
| Soft pruning, taking all but 2 leaves. Trim back in Aug. Branches may be developed by hard pruning technique | June. Covered wires | Light shade, burns easily | Early frost protection mandatory | Aphids | Medium depth; oval or rectangle |
| Soft pruning, taking all but 2 leaves. Branches may be developed by hard pruning technique | June. Covered wires | Light shade | Early frost protection mandatory | Aphids & scale | Simple oval or rectangle. Must have root run. Mound soil if shallow |
| Soft pruning, taking all but 2 leaves per shoot. Remove inner facing buds. Use sterile tools | June. Covered wires | Light shade, burns easily | Early frost protection mandatory | Relatively free | Medium to deep pots |
| Soft pruning, taking all but 2 leaves. Trim back in Aug. Branches may be developed by hard pruning technique | June. Covered wires | Light shade, burns easily | Early frost protection mandatory | Aphids & scale | Use deep containers. Simple oval or rectangle |
| Soft pruning & hard pruning technique. Prune to 1 bud if necessary | June. Covered wires | Light shade | Early frost protection mandatory | Some mealy bug. Fairly free | Medium to deep pots |
| Soft pruning, shoot & side leaf removal technique on vigorous trees. Branches: as for Elm | Mid-summer. Covered wires. Maples are brittle | Light shade & wind baffle | Early frost protection mandatory | Aphids & mildew | Simple oval or rectangle. Must have root run |
| Soft pruning, shoot & side leaf removal technique on vigorous trees. Branches: as for Elm | Mid-summer. Covered wires. Maples are brittle | Light shade & wind baffle | Early frost protection mandatory | Aphids & mildew | Simple oval or rectangle. Must have root run |
| Soft pruning, shoot & side leaf removal technique on vigorous trees. Branches: as for Elm | Mid-summer. Covered wires. Maples are brittle | Protect leaves until leather hard, otherwise they will 'fry' | Early frost protection mandatory | Aphids & mildew | Simple oval or rectangle. Must have root run |
| Soft pruning, it is necessary to thin out rather than bulk up | Mid-summer. Covered wires. Leaf trim prior to wiring clarifies. *Very* brittle | Light shade | Early frost protection mandatory | Aphids & mildew | Simple oval or rectangle. Must have root run |
| As for Mountain Maple, but shoot & side leaf removal technique is standard | Mid-summer. Covered wires. Leaf trimming prior to wiring clarifies | Light shade | Early frost protection mandatory | Aphids & mildew | Simple oval or rectangle. Must have root run |
| Soft pruning, taking all but 2 leaves. Leaf cut in May/June | June, covered wires | Light shade | Early frost protection mandatory | Aphids | Simple oval or rectangle. Must have root run. Mound soil if shallow |

# Cultural Data

| Species | Type and features | Repotting | Soil. Standard mix | Watering | Feeding | Branch pruning |
|---------|-------------------|-----------|--------------------|----------|---------|----------------|
| **FLOWERING & FRUITING TREES** | | | | | | |
| **Apricot** | Flowers on bare wood in Winter. Rough bark. Deciduous | After flowering. Feb./March. 1–4 yr according to age | Standard soil | Copiously during active growth. Year-round foliage misting keeps leaf colour. Spray flower *buds* | Cycle 5, feed A & B | Cut back after flowering |
| **Azalea, Satsuki** | Lanceolate green leaves. Immensely variable flowers. Evergreen | After flowering. May–July. Yearly or by root production | Standard soil with some expanded clay | Copiously during active growth. Year-round foliage misting keeps leaf colour | Cycle 5, feed B only at half strength | Cut back after flowering |
| **Cotoneaster** | Neat foliage, tiny pink flowers, red berries. Deciduous | March yearly or by observation | Standard soil with some expanded clay | Copiously | Cycle 5, feed A & B | March |
| **Crab Apple** | Pink/white flowers. Small fruit. Grey bark. Deciduous | October, 1–2 yr | Standard soil with some expanded clay | Copiously | Cycle 5, feed A & B | Cut back after flowering |
| **Firethorn** | Narrow foliage, clusters of white flowers, orange/red berries according to cv. Evergreen | March yearly or by observation | Standard soil with some expanded clay | Copiously | Cycle 5, feed A & B | August |
| **Hawthorn** | Cuneate foliage. Flowers white to red. Some bear fruit. Bark silvery. Deciduous | March yearly | Standard soil with some expanded clay | Copiously | Cycle 5, feed A & B | After flowering or fruiting season is over |
| **Holly, Deciduous** | Lanceolate foliage, white flowers, tiny red fruit. Silver grey bark | March 1–2 yr | Standard soil with some expanded clay | Copiously | Cycle 5, feed A & B | March |
| **Jasmine, Winter** | Narrow foliage, yellow flowers on bare wood late Winter. Deciduous | Yearly after flowering | Standard soil with some expanded clay | Copiously | Cycle 5, feed A & B | August |
| **Pomegranate** | Usually red flowers. Fruit in hot UK Summers. Fine leaves & fissured bark. Deciduous | March. 2–10 yr by root production | Standard soil with some expanded clay | Copiously | Cycle 5, feed A & B | Mid-summer |
| **Quince, Chinese** | Grown for form & bark display, & its yellow fruit. Flowers are pinky red. Deciduous | Autumn or Jan./Feb. when normal bud activity begins | Standard soil with some expanded clay | Evenly moist till fruits are obvious then water copiously | Cycle 5, feed A & B | Autumn |
| **Quince, Japanese** | Flowers on bare wood late Winter. Grey bark. Semi deciduous | October, 1–2 yr | Standard soil with some expanded clay | Copiously | Cycle 5, feed A & B | Cut back after flowering |
| **Spindle** | Lanceolate foliage, pink flowers/fruit. Red Autumn colour. Deciduous | March/Apr. yearly | Standard soil with a portion of expanded clay | Evenly moist. Ample water from flower to fruiting | Cycle 5, feed A & B | March |

| Pruning shoots | Wiring | Growing season placement | Dormant season placement | Pests | Containers |
|---|---|---|---|---|---|
| Trim long shoots in late Summer | Mid-summer. Covered wire. Brittle | Full sun | Early frost protection | Aphids | Medium to deep oval or rectangle |
| Soft pruning till mid June | Mid-summer. Covered wire. Brittle | Full sun | Early frost protection | Aphids | Medium to deep oval or rectangle |
| Soft pruning to 2 pairs of leaves. Branches may be developed by hard pruning technique. Reduce opposite limbs | Spring to Summer. Wire new growth. Old limbs brittle | Full sun | Early frost protection | Aphids & mealy bug | Medium to deep oval or rectangle |
| Prune new shoots early & leave till Aug. trimback | Spring to Summer. Covered wire | Full sun | Early frost protection | Aphids & root Aphids | Medium to deep oval or rectangle |
| Pinch new shoots to 2 pairs of leaves in Spring | Spring through Summer. As for Cotoneaster | Full sun | Early frost protection | Aphids & mealy bug | Medium to deep oval or rectangle |
| As for Crab Apple | Mid-summer. Covered wire. Brittle | Full sun | Early frost protection | Aphids & mealy bug | Medium to deep oval or rectangle |
| Remove extraneous material early. Pinch back to 2 pairs of leaves | Mid-summer. Covered wire. Brittle | Full sun | Early frost protection | Aphids & mealy bug | Medium to deep oval or rectangle |
| Cut primary shoots in June. Wire secondary shoots when they reach 15 cm (6 in) length | Mid-summer. Covered wire. Brittle | Full sun | Early frost protection | Aphids & mealy bug | Medium to deep oval or rectangle |
| Soft prune long shoots. Examine short ones for apically borne flowers | Spring to Summer. Covered wire | Full sun | Early frost protection. Keep warm through Winter | Aphids and root Aphids | Medium to deep oval or rectangle |
| Soft pruning till mid-June | Mid-summer. Covered wire. Brittle | Full sun | Early frost protection | Aphids & mealy bug | Medium to deep oval or rectangle |
| Trim long shoots in late Summer | Spring to Summer. Covered wire | Full sun | Early frost protection | Nematodes & aphids | Medium to deep oval or rectangle |
| Prune shoots after flowers show | Mid-summer. Covered wire. Brittle | Full sun | Early frost protection | Aphids & mealy bug | Medium to deep oval or rectangle |

# Index

## Index